DROPPING IN ON THE WAVES OF LIFE

A Guide for Young Adults

Peter McBride

*I dedicate this book to those who, like myself, lack a
bit of common sense, and may not have the family
and friends around them enough to provide guidance
through the many many close calls ahead.*

CONTENTS

Adolescent anxiety & depression

PREFACE

(Or why reading this book is a good idea!)

I'm a surfer. I have the patience to sit on my board waiting for the waves to come so I can "drop in" on a wave and ride it to its end. But I don't always have the patience required to wade through the reading of prefaces, especially ten-page ones. I know these introductions can provide you, the reader, with clues as to what to expect. Maybe you like that. Maybe you don't think you need the guidance. Either way, it's the value or message you take away from these stories which matters, and this preface will help.

Living and learning from life is like surfing. You catch many different "waves", you live through so many experiences. You need to understand that the quality, the joy and thrill of your rides, that life you lead, depend upon the size and form of each "wave" of your life. Certainly, your wave-riding knowledge and ability help. This book aims to help you develop that ability.

This is NOT a book of short stories about surfing. Undoubtedly, every surfer could write an entertaining book about adventures on their boards, in the ocean and at the beach. I might write one, eventually. And yes, surfing definitely does occur multiple times throughout these chapters, but this book serves another purpose...

The idea behind this book is to share with you both the successes and the mistakes you may encounter through examples from my own life. I've chosen to drop in on some really great waves (read: experiences), and I've also chosen to go for those where a wipeout is inevitable. My hope is, through reading my stories, you might attain some signals, some alerts, and perhaps avoid some of the errors I've made.

Whether you are male or female, non-binary, or undecided, whether you live near the coast or inland, and regardless of your ethnic or religious background, chances are you'll do some of the same goofy stuff I did. It's part of living life. Every day is different, which can bring on changes in you. There is the thrill of a great day out on your board where the waves and your ability connect perfectly, only to return the next morning to the disappointment of crummy conditions where the waves are flat, and you're bummed out. Or worse, the waves are perfect, but the next day you keep falling off and can't make anything work. That's also part of life.

No doubt you've had these kinds of days.

I hope you'll dip into the following chapters, each a story about a particular time in my life and look at the comments (Second Thoughts) and questions (Dropping In Deeper) that follow. They've been added to provide some additional perspective, and to help you develop some empathy as to how much we all have in common. Think of me as your own little "Jiminy Cricket" perched on your shoulder – I hope you've seen "Pinocchio!" If not, picture a little fella there, whispering to you a wee bit of advice. I can help you avoid some of the pitfalls and little tricky situations awaiting you out in this World* of ours.

Then, go out and drop in on your own waves as you ride through all the new adventures, miracles, missteps, and mishaps in life, and come to know the joys, challenges, and lessons in the greatest surf adventure (surfari) of them all -- your life.

*Throughout the book, I capitalize "World" purposely, just as I do "Earth." It's a wonderous place.

To the teachers in the crowd...

No one expects students to answer all of the questions which follow each chapter. Choose several you find appropriate for your class and use those to help determine comprehension levels. The "sketch as your mind's eye sees it" questions can be responded to with "stick" figures and loose drawings. This is not an art test. But the artwork and captions reveal how well the students envision incidents in the stories - a reflection of reading comprehension. Some of the other questions could help initiate class discussions and again provide a window into the readers' interpretations and potential for learning from the incidents described.

The whole process could make reading this book even more meaningful and fun! And that's the point.

Chapter 1: Sheila In
Red - *Infatuation, Love Triangles & Friendship*

As a kid, my world can be summed up in two words: "Right" and "Wrong." Things that you do are either Right or Wrong and everything has consequences. At six years old, for example, I know that smacking my little brother is wrong and I will get punished. Sometimes that means getting my dad's leather belt to my bottom. He never punishes when he's angry. He just gets the point across by telling me how many it'll be this time – two, three, bare bottom or not. He's not cruel or vindictive; he's just the enforcer. Unlike today, in the 1950s many people considered this form of discipline acceptable. Usually, my mom reports the infraction and Dad takes care of things when he gets home from work. It can't be very rewarding being Dad in these instances.

At ten years old I know that "forgetting" to take out the trash is wrong, and there goes this week's allowance. I lose the chance to put anything into my savings account, buy a candy bar or go to the movies. But the next week I remember, and everything is as it should be.

As a teen, at 14 years old, I know not turning in my English composition is wrong, and my grades will suffer. My dignity suffers as well, especially if I'm the only one in class who hasn't turned in the assignment. I get better and better over time at getting the work completed. The consequences are usually clear.

I have so many opportunities to choose to do the right thing. Life is fairly simple. I know where I stand and, while each day brings a challenge, I have a lot of fun as well. It's likely I can't appreciate all the certainty about life at this point. Later, I will look back and realize how special my youth has been.

Now I'm 16. I'm in high school. My 10' Con surfboard fits perfectly inside my baby blue '56 Chevy Nomad panel truck. The mattress in the back makes sleeping at the beach easier. Gone are the pre-car days of sleeping over at the beach, lying in my sleeping bag on the sand by a dying fire with the nose of my surfboard tucked under me so no one can steal it. Life is good now…except things are about to become more complicated. "Right" and "Wrong" are still a part of my world, but I'm about to learn "It Depends" as well.

At 16, here's the "Right" part of my world. Sheila. She's a very attractive blonde whose eyes remind me of an impish elf. She understands how to use just the perfect amount of makeup – quite sophisticated for her age. Sheila's in one of the unofficial girls' social clubs at school, the Atamets, and she has dated a lot. She's very popular. She even has her own landline phone and phone number, which is unique these days. Oh, and she's a semester ahead of me and models for Bullock's Wilshire, a high-end department store. I've been infatuated with her since that day back in junior high when I first saw her in a red blouse.

It's June at the close of my second year of high school, but I still have never spoken to Sheila. I don't think she's even aware of me, but I have become a kind of a teenage stalker, I guess. Understand, I don't mean any harm. I just manage to figure out when she will be heading down the main stairway for a break. Most days I can position myself to be walking up the stairs at the same time, books in my left hand, just hoping, somehow, she might brush by on the way down. Occasionally it works! That thrill of her possibly touching me, along with the challenges of football or swimming practice each day after class, make school a great place to be!

Here's the "Wrong" part of my world: Ron. Ron is my friend. I surf with him and the guys on weekends at County Line. He's a very good surfer, super popular, fun, and always up to great mischief. I must admit he's handsome, too, more so than me. Ron has even included me on his family's surf trips to Mexico. What can be "Wrong" about that? Well, he happens to be... Sheila's boyfriend. Kind of.

Ron doesn't hang out with her at school. He'd rather be with the guys. He doesn't pay that much attention to her in public. But everyone knows they are a couple.

One early summer Saturday I'm in the café at County Line Beach, about eighteen miles up the coast from Malibu. It's right across the Coast Highway from the ocean. I have just finished surfing and I'm barefoot with nothing on but my surf trunks. Patches of gray-white sand spot my chest and elbows and my trunks are still rather dripping wet. My hair looks like a wave that just exploded on the shore. I don't care. I'm rich. Not only do I have gas money to get back home, but there's a dollar in the pocket of my trunks (where usually there's only a bar of surf wax) for a cup of tea and a bag of Barbecue Fritos! The tea is perfect because you can keep getting refills of hot water and pour on the sugar. It lasts forever.

I've just bought the chips and tea and turn around from the counter when I see her. She's sitting with some other girls in one of the booths by the front windows! Sheila! There she twinkles with her movie star looks as the picture window beside her makes the Coast Highway and bluff overlooking the beach a backdrop for her movie. Her appearance there is a long-held fantasy come true! I see her long platinum blonde hair all flowing down to one side across her raging red bikini top. She smiles and her dimples' cheerful "Hello" shares the warmth of her doe eyes so blue. But what's she doing here? This is not the kind of beach girls like to go to because of its kelp-strewn rocks and kelp flies swarming around them. Besides, world-famous Malibu Beach is much closer to home for her.

It's everything I can do to keep myself from getting "excited." A cup of tea and chips aren't going to camouflage anything. I'm acutely aware of this.

And you know what? Sheila looks over, actually notices me, our eyes connect, and she motions for me to come over to the table to sit with her and her girlfriends! Whoa! What's a guy to do? Is it "Wrong?" No, this is heaven. I move in like a missile as she slides over to make room on the green vinyl booth seat, and there I am. I can feel the warmth, her warmth, emanating from the soft plastic which had been so lucky to lie beneath her. Our knees are touching! There's no way I can explain it, but my heart beats so powerfully I'm feeling a pain in my side. I'm living a moment I will treasure my entire life. I know it. Please make it last.

Why she is here I don't know. I don't care! Everything is so great!

Here you need to know something about me. From fifth to ninth grade, I attended an all-boys school. With two brothers and no sisters, my knowledge about girls could fill the ingredients label on a bag of salted peanuts. I can't dance. If I'm on the phone with a girl, I have to place beside me a list of possible topics — e.g., the football game, the principal's announcement that girls can't wear culottes (a skirt with shorts), or whether Bob's Drive-In really does put a whole piece of cheese in the cheeseburger — in case the conversation begins to lag. Last of all, I lack self-confidence.

But there is hope. I surf, I play football and I'm on the swim team. These give me some "creds" with everyone. I have some buddies I know and surf with, and I have the reputation of being a good surfer – and a true surfer, not a "summer surfer". I'm one of those guys in the water all year long, even when the air is 55 degrees, and the water is the same. Our boards weigh about 35 pounds and wetsuits for surfing don't exist. Oh, and we have no leash on our surfboards, so when we fall off, they wash all the way to shore onto the rocky beach.

I don't have a girlfriend. Maybe that's obvious. At this point, I've only been on one real date in my whole life, and that was before I could drive. It only happened because one day while I was outside during a break at summer school, a girl typed "I love you" on my typewriter. I figured out who it was and thought maybe I could ask her about doing something together. After our movie date, with my dad in the car waiting to take me home, I walked her to her back door. The lights were out but I didn't even have the nerve to kiss her goodnight. She was really pretty, too! I just didn't think she would want me to kiss her. Likewise, I figured she wouldn't want to go out with me again.

Why a girl like Sheila, so out of my league, would want to talk to me is beyond anything I know or understand. But I don't care. Bring it on! This feels "Right." Then, somewhere in the middle of these precious moments with Sheila and her friends she turns to me and asks, "Are you doing anything tonight?"

"Am I doing anything? No! Why?"

"The Atamets are having a party tonight and I wondered if you'd like to go with me."

"What about Ron?" I ask with a bit of confusion mixed with intense interest in my voice.

"What about him?" she responds.

I remember he doesn't give her much attention. So, I figure, what the heck. "Sure," I say.

And that's all it takes for me to end a two-year friendship with my surf buddy, Ron, you know, the guy who's been on the swim team with me, who sneaks his mom's car sometimes so the two of us can skip swim practice and chase waves, and who's helped make my days in high school ever so memorable - just like that. Poof! Amazing!

Now, he's not perfect. He does talk behind your back sometimes, making you the brunt of some joking of his…but it's understood that you take the lumps with the gravy. The friendship with Ron is a lot more gravy than gristle. I do him wrong by accepting her invitation but accept it I do! She gives me her phone number and address, tells me to pick her up around eight, and I'm all set!

When I get back home from the beach that afternoon, I'm so excited! Time crawls as I wait for dusk and the short drive to Sheila's home. I manage to clean myself up pretty nicely for the night's adventure. Finally, eventually, wonderfully, as evening dawns, I'm behind the wheel and steering my way to new territory. This is the girl I have fantasized about for a couple of years! She's the second date of my life and the first without my dad driving. I know I'm looking pretty good. I'm all tan, my hair, bleached blonde by the sun, looks good…combed.

I arrive at her house in my baby blue Chevy Nomad panel truck - it's basically a station wagon designed for deliveries with solid panels where the rear windows should be. I have that mattress in the back I sleep on at the beach, and I'm ready for whatever the Fates will allow. Don't misunderstand me. I've only kissed one girl in my whole life, and that was for one brief moment at a church youth meeting in junior high. I plan to wait until I'm married for anything really serious. But I'm quite willing to explore just how close I can get! The mattress might work out for something like that — someday. I can dream.

I pull up, pop out, and zip to her door. Sheila answers the doorbell. She's ready. She looks so scrumptious. At the first sight of her, I'm overwhelmed with her beauty, and my eyes open so wide I must look like I'm witnessing a car accident, which of course isn't the look I'm going for. She's in red, which so wonderfully complements that long platinum blonde hair. She has that smile…oh man, I know it will remain in my memory coils forever. And her perfume, undoubtedly from Bullocks Wilshire, envelops me like fog, her fog, and I'm flying with Peter Pan, thinking my "happy thoughts". I treasure this moment. Ron? Who's Ron? Don't know the guy.

I'm all set to whisk her away to whatever kind of party it's going to be. I figure I'll know some people there from school and manage. Sure, I'm self-conscious about my dancing abilities – I still try to make perfect squares when I'm doing the box-step while slow dancing, but I'm beginning to accept that's it's okay to "cheat" a bit and glide more than stride. I'm up for the evening, whatever it entails!

Then Sheila throws me a slider. "Let's just stay here! I'll make you a Coke and we can talk." She leaves and walks into the kitchen to mix custom Cokes for us (Coke syrup and soda water). I'm telling you, she has her own phone, she makes her own Cokes, she's beautiful...I've found, okay...stumbled upon, the perfect girl.

"Um...okay."

This is the first and only step we ever take together in our "relationship." It will become our routine. She opens her front door, welcoming me into the living room. It's dimly lit. A comfy couch stands at the ready...an aqua aura radiates from a gently gurgling aquarium where one little fish scoots around happily. She doesn't pay it any attention, but it's a cute little thing. She gestures for me to take my seat on the couch and heads to the kitchen to prepare the drinks. Pretty nifty! I'm in Sheila's home. I'm sitting on her couch. I'm in ecstasy.

Have you ever gone fishing? Sometimes fishermen use lures instead of live bait to hook a fish. Remember the feeling at the first hit as the fish tries to leap, yank, and struggle to get away? I do. It's truly thrilling. Now, have you ever caught a fish that doesn't put up much of a fight, it sort of gives up as you drag it in and just flops lamely onto the deck when you pull it out of the water? I have. It's rather disappointing, almost boring.

I'm one of those fish. You figure out which one. There I sit, in Sheila's living room. She returns with two Cokes. I'm of the mindset that whatever she says, goes. It's not long before I'm making out with her. I'd always wondered about whether noses get in the way when you're kissing. Somehow, they don't. This is my very first make-out session. It's soon to be followed by my second, third, and so on for the next two months of that summer. Sheila teaches me well. If my hand begins to wander, she guides it back home. She won't accept any messing around, I guess. I see her about once a week…always at her place…her mom stays way back in the bedroom. We never go anywhere. I'm a happy fish, like the lucky one in her little fish tank.

It's kind of tough at the beach. Everybody knows. Guys I surf with say, "How could you do that to Ron?" It turns out he's talking to everyone I know about what a backstabber I am. I can't deny it. But I don't think the term quite fits. It depends on how you look at the matter. I figure he should be giving her more of his attention. When we happen to be surfing in the same spot, he kicks his surfboard in my direction to hit me. I take it for a while and then finally go after him one afternoon in the parking lot and challenge him to a fight, but he backs away and jumps in his car. Things are really ugly. But thoughts of Sheila make everything okay.

Nothing lasts forever. My friendship with Ron certainly doesn't. In similar fashion, with the passing of a couple of summer months, Sheila's interest in me begins to wane. It doesn't help when, like a dummy, I leave Sheila's phone number in a place my mom can find it. One evening when I've been over there for a bit longer than usual, Mom calls Sheila to make sure I'm okay since I haven't yet arrived home. Her mom picks up the phone and comes into our little love nest to announce that my mom needs to speak to me. It's kind of hard to get back into the mood after such an interruption. Things change. Over the next week or so when I call, Sheila's "not home," or no one answers. This is something new.

But I do go over again. This time it isn't scheduled, I just drop by. She's home! She lets me in. Oh boy, and she's all dressed up and looking as great as when I first came over! We're talking about things and I realize she's not gesturing for me to sit down. I'm concerned. I know I'm in love…she's my dream come true… she's everything a guy could want…THERE'S A KNOCK AT THE

DOOR!

Sheila immediately leaves me to open it. She turns the knob, pulls the door open, and voila! There stands Ron! He's dressed for the kill. I'm headed for the slaughter.

I stand for a moment avoiding eye contact with Ron and look to Sheila asking, no, pleading with my eyes, "Who should leave?" After all, my mantra has always been that whatever she says, goes.

"I think you should go."

I guess that floppy fish she effortlessly landed on the deck has now begun to smell. I leave her house, its comfortable, gurgling fish tank sound fades away as I shuffle down her path, in the opposite direction I would desire. I manage to bumble my way into my panel truck and drive away, never to be seen there again.

My tears fall. This is my first broken heart. It's the one just before my second broken heart, which is the one just before my third broken heart. Do understand, this goes both ways, as my journey through life also creates unintended heartbreak for some women I come to know. I am to learn that loving involves heartbreak, and you feel like it's the end of everything…for a while. But with time, the weather changes, the clouds go away, and the sun shines again over new times, new people, new experiences. This is SO important to understand! We ALL go through this at one point or another, that is, if we truly love someone. Your first experience may sadly be a relative, even a mom or dad, sister or brother. Having a pet and going through that feeling of loss when it dies prepares us for these times as well. Being a friend to someone who is going through heartbreak can be so valuable and meaningful to everyone involved.

In time I think back about what has happened. I begin to realize why Sheila never wanted to go anywhere except her house. I figure out why we never did attend that Atamets party at the start. Are you thinking what I'm thinking?

Yup, I was an unwitting shill. I helped her make Ron jealous enough to show more interest! I became that little ignored fish swimming around in her aquarium. But I can't deny I was having a great time! I can't deny she gave me the opportunity to be someone important to her. I just wasn't up to the task. I can't deny she truly is out of my league, and I pretty well knew that right from the start. Worst of all, I can't deny my willingness to take the risk and betray a good friend for the opportunity.

Was it worth it? Is this something I would repeat if I could? I don't know. All I know is I will never forget...Sheila in red.

Second Thoughts

※

Friendships are precious. In life, we only make a limited number of truly best friends. The word "make" means you must work at that kind of friendship. Friendship means love. Yet the author is willing to abandon a good friend, possibly a best friend, in pursuit of what he believes to be love. The "It depends" part of "Right" and "Wrong" clearly appears in his story. At times like these in life, it helps to talk to someone with experience about what is happening to you, what you are going through. Maybe that could be your mom or dad. But you may be saying to yourself, "I don't know anyone who could give me guidance like that." If that is the case, it is your job, your responsibility, to seek out such a person to include in your life NOW before you are put to the test.

Dropping In Deeper

Some questions are included at the end of each chapter, giving you a chance to see how my experiences might apply to your own life, and to provide the "practice time" to explore your thoughts and feelings with each new situation. There's no time like the present to dig into your feelings. It may affect those "Right and Wrong" choices at the moment they're occurring. These questions can also be shared with your friends. Maybe they're feeling some of the same things.

1. Why are our childhood years so special?

2. Why does the author find it hard to talk to girls?

3. Why do you think Sheila decides they should just stay at her house instead of going to the club party together?

4. Imagine the author is a girl who attended an all-girls school much of her life, and who has no brothers, just sisters. Do you think she would have a difficult time talking to boys? Why or why not?

5. What does it mean to be "self-conscious" as in "...self-conscious about my dancing..."? Use the word "self-concious" in a sentence.

6. Do you believe the author is truly "in love" with Sheila? How do you know? What other word or words could be used to describe how he feels?

7. Why does the author betray his friendship with Ron and accept Sheila's invitation?

8. Sometimes art can help capture a feeling or idea. You don't need to be an artist but try and sketch the author's view as he first makes eye contact with Sheila at the café as your mind's eye sees it OR when the author is sleeping on the beach at County Line. Be sure to include a caption to describe the picture.

9. Do you think that what happened was partly Ron's fault? Describe a time in your life when you may have not given the proper attention to someone.

10. Do you think a broken heart is quite possible with "first love?" Does this happen to almost everyone at some time? If your heart gets broken someday, what can you do for yourself until time finally helps you get over it?

Chapter 2: The Avalon Monster – *Dealing With Fear & Loneliness*

A twelve-year-old boy's brain isn't even halfway to full development – very little for a scientist to probe or explore. Its mass is about a pound, weight about 500 grams. The depth of its convolutions, those wrinkles of the brain we all see in pictures – also known as gyri, can't be much over the thickness of his all-time best book report – all two and a half pages, double-spaced.

Ill-equipped as he may be, however, the boy ventures out into this grand World of ours, undaunted and unafraid.

A bonus for him is how his twenty-four-hour day goes by. So

much is brand new and, every day, his awareness of the World around him expands. Experiences don't clump together as they will later in life when one encounter may seem familiar and similar to others. As a result, time passes at a crawl. Any celebration — Christmas, Hanukkah, Eid al-Adha, or a birthday — seems to take forever to finally arrive.

And there is extra free time which can lead to self-discovery as those urges of adolescence begin to poke their way into each of his days. At this point, maybe it's a perfect time to go off to summer camp.

One summer, at age 12, in the midst of this wonderfully tumultuous period of life, my parents send me to YMCA camp on Catalina Island off the Southern California coast.

Let me paint you a picture: the camp is set on a beach at the far end of a cove, surrounded on two sides by steeply rising hillsides. A canyon lies behind it. This is the east side of the island, facing the California coast, so open-ocean waves don't form. Next to the beach, there are maybe a half-dozen rectangular, raised-off-the ground tents with vaulted canvas roofs and open sides. After all, Southern California is notorious for little or no rain in summer. With a warm climate like this, the open-air sides seem quite practical, most of the time, for the campers in their six bunk beds underneath the canvas.

The floor of the tent is crafted from scratchy planks and all of this, supported on the four corners by 18-inch-high cut sections of old coal tar-covered telephone poles, rests upon dirt. Next to the tents, the pebble-strewn beach stretches 100 feet to the cove's calm waters. The hillsides are covered in chaparral, cactus, and an occasional tree. Visible wildlife consists of seabirds, squirrels, some roaming wild boars back in the canyons, and the bees and flies.

To give you an idea of how close the tents are to the ocean, I can throw a pebble from the tent and reach the water. The cove, maybe 200 yards across and about the same distance to where it opens to the sea, is all ours. No other camps or homes are in the area.

When I take the two steps up to enter the tent there is always a creaking sound on that first one. Inside are six sets of military-style, two-bed bunks, a sleeping bag and pillow on top of each, with an open aisle running down the center.

This is before the advent of personal injury attorneys advertising their "Larry Parker got me five million dollars" accident lawsuits, so supervision is very casual. Rowboats are issued to groups of four 12-year-olds who take them out. An adult supervises somewhere in the vicinity, but certainly not on every boat. We enjoy the splashing oar-wars on the way out to go snorkeling.

My major interest is in the sea life: colorful fish of all kinds, especially bright orange and protected garibaldi, scary moray eels, and elusive, so far to me, abalone. I also have the amazing made-by-my-own-hands Hawaiian sling spear comprised of surgical tubing, string, a nailed-on 5-prong spearhead, and wooden pole from the camp store. With my mask, snorkel, and fins, I am a potential threat to anything in the water, other than wildlife. I will admit that the only fish I ever "catch" in my three years of spearfishing at camp is a sedentary sea slug resting on the sandy ocean bottom. But the potential for disaster is everywhere. This is such a great time!

Back to the tents — any veteran of summer camp knows to always take the top bunk. One reason is that the guy on the bottom bunk might otherwise have to suffer an "Ernie" residing above him.

My first year, I encounter an "Ernie" on the very first night. I have chosen a bottom bunk. Clearly, I'm not in the know. In the middle of night darkness, the whole bunk starts shaking, waking me up. Little Ernie up above mumbles, "Gotta go to the bathroom. Gotta go to the bathroom!"

The tent counselor comes to the rescue and helps the fella down, but not before Ernie steps on my arm. The waving flashlight in my eyes reminds me that I'm awake and not dreaming. Though most of us manage it by ourselves, Ernie waddles off to the "Queen" (our nickname for the bathroom a couple of hundred feet away) with the counselor. Apparently, Ernie requires special attention. He does seem a bit goofy and immature. There is a 75-watt bulb at the bathroom door to guide them. It's just enough.

I doze for a few minutes until, upon Ernie's return, I'm rudely awakened again. He steps on my leg while climbing back up onto his bunk. As nights go by, this becomes a routine.

For this and other reasons, in the following summers, I always choose the upper berth!

While the camp store sells necessities such as soap and craft supplies, it also provides another must for survival – candy. For obvious reasons, especially with all the bugs and varmints around, we are told, "Do not take candy into the tent." But someone, usually one of the new guys, always does.

After dinner in the dining hall, each day ends as darkness creeps in, with everyone together at the campfire. One tent is responsible for gathering the wood and stacking it to be burned. It is a primitive area that might exaggeratingly be called an "amphitheater." Cut telephone poles are set in the dirt long-ways for seating and there is a rock-encircled fire pit in front. There is no real pit, just dirt and ashes on the flat ground. No lights, no concrete, and no "This Way Back to Camp" or emergency exit signs exist. It's just a simple gathering site. It's perfect.

One tent team builds the fire. On some nights the fire is great while on others it's rather wimpy. A counselor plays guitar while leading in the singing of folksongs such as "John Jacob Jingle Heimer Schmidt." Between songs and announcements, other tents present skits for all the campers to enjoy. The skits revolve around themes such as stupid bullies losing out or silly teachers making mistakes or soldiers needing toilet paper.

As the evening ends, one of the leaders begins to tell a tale. Somehow, someway, he always seems to be able to time the ending of the story to the last dying ember of the fire crumbling and extinguishing. In the chill and black of night, we all trudge back to our tents, flashlights ablaze as we blind one another with them. It is wonderful to look back and realize everyone always makes it back to their tent! I don't know how it happens!

I remember one particular story told by our camp leader, Juan. He's standing in front of the fire pit as a piece of a branch drops into the embers, momentarily flaring up and brightening the back of his jacket – we basically see his silhouette, his face obscured in the shadow of night.

He speaks in a low, whispery voice. We strain to hear as we lean forward, not a peep from us.

> *"Years ago, an older couple in Avalon (the only town on Catalina Island, a few miles away from our camp) had always wanted a child, but for some reason never could have one. They went to doctor after doctor for assistance, but it didn't help.*
>
> *One day the wife read an ad in the paper about a visitor*

from India who was a specialist in herbs and special medicines. He claimed to have special ground-up roots to help with almost any medical problem. She called him and secretly made an appointment. Her visit was brief. She told of their problem bearing a child – the visitor from India reached up on a shelf and brought down a twisted tiny branch, about the size of a child's hand. Without saying a word, he took a knife, scraped off three tiny shavings and then put them in a small pot of boiling water for a minute.

He then poured the hot liquid into a strangely marked black cup and handed it to her. "You will have a child." She drank.

Nine months later she gave birth to the couple's dream-come-true child they had awaited so many years. But the attending nurse gasped in horror. The dream was now the nightmare of a twisted and deformed baby boy: eyes out of place, arms almost to its knees, shrieking and covered in moldy brown hair – but very alive."

…The campfire burns lower and lower as our faces get dimmer and dimmer. Nobody blinks, and all is silent for a moment but for the shifting of a crumbling ember…

The couple took the child home and hid it. They had this old-fashioned belief that it must be some kind of curse placed upon them for doing something wrong, so they didn't want anyone to know. As time passed and the creature developed, they moved it into the underground basement in a cage with a hinged door in front and the bare concrete wall in back.

They hired a keeper to take care of it.

Over the years it grew, and it developed a habit of digging at the concrete wall at the back of the cage. Its fingernails, now solid orange, looked more like shards of colored glass than anything human. The scratch marks dug deeper and deeper over time, and the creature made horrible noises, especially in the night.

The keeper treated the creature like it was a vicious animal – throwing its food through the cage opening, using the hose to both soak the creature and clean up the cage floor, and taunting it day by day. This continued for years as it grew.

As time passed the creature appeared and sounded more like a huge Tasmanian devil than a human. It continued to dig at the wall in the night.

Then late one night the keeper carelessly came too close to the cage. The last sound he ever heard was
RARHHHHH

We all jump as the teller of the tale screams in the creature's voice! He resumes telling the story.

In an instant the keeper saw white, then darkness. The keys to the cage soon changed hands.

Meanwhile, the couple rested upstairs, and a while later, in the darkness, heard the creaking of a step on the stairway. The husband called into the darkness, 'Who's there?'

That was the next to the last sound either of them ever

heard.

Days later police found their mangled bodies and the open cage, but no creature.

You heard about that guy about a month ago in Avalon who was found savagely murdered, right?"

(Of course, the guy next to me nods, "Yes." My eyes get that wide-eyed Little Orphan Annie look.)

"Well, it seems there have been other night murders recently. One was reported near the Boy Scout camp not far from here. Just thought you should know."

With that, as the embers make a last gasp, we stand up in the darkness as one of the counselors takes out his guitar and leads a closing song, "Kumbaya." It's pitiful. I mean, our voices sound more like the warbling moan of a sick kid late at night calling, "Mommmmm…"

Then off we trudge, flashlights torching through the darkness, as if that might help, to our open-air tents.

I head to the Queen with a gang of other guys (strength in numbers). I make it through brushing my teeth, find my way back to the tent, roll into my bed, and pull the covers over my head. I can hear the crackled recording of "Taps" being played, as is the custom each night, as we fall asleep. But this time it sounds more like a "Goodbye." The music takes on a whole new meaning. No way am I ready for sleep. I can't close my eyes. It's not a good idea. I must keep vigilant…

But I guess I fade off because somewhere in the night my bunk shakes me awake. I'm startled, too scared to look. I squeeze my eyes tighter but then welcome Ernie's, "I gotta go to the bathroom!" as he gets up.

"Thank you, Ernie," I whisper to myself. That was kind of close.

So, the counselor once again leads him to the Queen, and I rest a moment. But almost immediately, there's a different noise.

First, there's that familiar creak of the step leading to the tent. But it's too soon for Ernie and the counselor's return. Then there's some kind of a shuffling, scuffling sound!

Did you ever grasp the lip of a heavy potted plant to drag it to a nearby spot, and then feel that jolt of sharp pain as your toe gets pinched because you've forgotten to keep it well ahead of the moving base of the pot?

Imagine that feeling turned into fright. Somebody shouts, "Avalon Monster!" as I hear it scrape along in our tent, no doubt planning to devour us!

I can hear its heavy breathing. I can smell its foul odors and oozings. I can't see it because I'm cowering deep inside my sleeping bag and naturally my eyes are glued shut for protection. And anyway, it's dark.

Every one of us is awake now. We scream. We make scared little peeping noises. There's the ruffle of more sleeping bags being pulled over heads for protection from the monster.... we lie there still as coffins. Every little kid believes that if we're under the covers and in a protective fetal position, eyes closed, we'll be safe...sort of...

Then one of the guys calls out, "Wild boar!"

Yes, we are dealing with a wild boar making snouting noises

as it works its way through the canvas-topped cabin. Its hot "garlic-on-my-salad" breath nails those unfortunates, like myself, resting on the bottom bunks! Suddenly, the half-eaten Hershey bar and wrapper on the floor below one of the bunks disappears, and so does the boar!

I work up the gumption to open my eyes and pull the covers from over my head.

Just about then Ernie and the counselor return. Guys are talking all at once. But soon we settle down. The searchlight effect of a half-dozen flashlight beams fades away, and it's back to sleep for some.

The arrival of Morning Light takes forever. We have a lot to talk about at breakfast. Nobody wants to admit we thought the boar was a monster. We keep that to ourselves.

The next night, just after campfire, we get brave and go for an "Iron Man Swim" in the cove. It's pitch dark with no moon, and the water looks like coffee, black and still.

The counselors encourage us all to wade out and swim the 25 yards to the floating platform. It has a slide and is lit by that familiar 75-watt spotlight. Some of the campers opt-out because it is a bit chilly and swimming in the dark ocean is not for them. But I'm up for it.

I don't think the bottom is any more than 10 feet deep, and that's only out at the platform. There's enough room on that platform for ten kids to stand at one time while waiting for the slide. Safety is not an issue for us. After all, nylon ropes with floats surround the swim area so we don't get lost in the darkness.

Possibly fifty of us are churning up the water this late evening.

After messing around and never quite managing to climb up on the platform because of the crowd, I work my way back, off to the side, right along the perimeter rope.

By myself and in my own little section of the swim area, the water is now about waist deep and my feet slide about on the cobblestones and sandy bottom. I want to head to shore.

I look over my shoulder toward the distant mouth of the cove. Out past the swimming platform and to the left something is moving, in the water, not on it. It's darker than the rest of the ocean water and seems to be coming in my direction!

I'm paralyzed as it advances, now definitely heading towards me!

Avalon Monster feeling! I'm trying to utter something, anything, a warning…no, not really a warning. I'm too frightened to be concerned about anyone except myself. But with all of the clamor from the guys elsewhere in the water whatever sound I make is indiscernible and not loud enough.

The darkness sweeps in. This is for real! I am not imagining this! I am actually being swept up by this darkness and maybe no one will even notice I've disappeared until sometime later in the night.

The darkness envelops my little legs. I can feel it. It's grabbing, no, poking my legs. My time is up, and this is the end.

It's sort of a swarming darkness. It passes around me and journeys next to the shore where it stops and changes direction. But instead of this Avalon Monster going up onto the beach, raising its ugly head to climb out and seek poor little victims in the camp, the dark mass moves on in the water down the beach. My life will continue.

I never relate this experience to anyone. It's something at this age I have no ability to articulate or explain to anyone. My buddies would just think I'm nuts. I'm just so glad to still be alive.

A number of years later, late one evening while on a beach with a girlfriend, I see that same darkness in the water again. I finally resolve the mystery of my Iron Man Swim at camp so many years before, when I thought I saw the monster in the water. I realize this underlying fear of something I had never resolved or understood had concerned me all these years – running in my subconscious like a background app! The "monster" had only been grunion, tiny little ocean fish which at certain times of the year swim up to shore to lay their eggs!

All that time I kept that worry that something bad might happen at bay as best I could without knowing any explanation of what it was. Now I realize that learning to cope with that fear made me stronger.

The Avalon Monster, for all of us, will return again and again in our lives, sometimes when it's dark, or when we're alone, or something out of the ordinary takes place. We all have unarticulated or unexplained fears. In life, it's all a matter of how we handle them. We must find a way to cope with this Avalon Monster feeling, understanding that it will never completely go away.

Second Thoughts

※

Isn't it funny how you can be in a tent with eleven other people, or in the water with fifty, and yet feel so alone? In life, you can be surrounded by others who care about you and often share the same problems you face, but you don't turn to them for help. We're in this Life together. We all need to remember that and to look to one another for assistance. TELL SOMEONE IF YOU'RE WORRIED OR TROUBLED! DON'T KEEP IT IN!

Find someone who will listen to your concerns and fears…. a close friend, family member, religious leader, teacher, or counselor. Then again, you might find someone out there seeking your help, as well!

Handled the right way, The Avalon Monster can just be something that keeps life… interesting.

Dropping In Deeper

1. According to the story, how does a young child experience life compare to the way an older person experiences life?

2. Why does the couple in the story keep their child a secret?

3. Sketch the tent with its bunk beds in it as your mind's eye sees it OR the campfire site OR the Avalon Monster in his cage. Describe your picture with a caption.

4. What does "gumption" mean as in "...work up the gumption to open my eyes..."? Use it in a sentence.

5. If you were older than me at the time, maybe 18 years old, and you were told this story in the same situation, do you think you would be as frightened? Why or why not?

6. Would this be a story you are likely to hear at an all-girls camp? Why or why not?

7. What is the main lesson of this story? Explain.

8. Describe a time when you have told someone about a worry or fear you have or tell of a time you wish you had told someone about a problem.

Chapter 3: Smokey –
The Value Of Friendship

J ohn's a buddy of mine. We meet in junior high when I'm about 14. I wish I could recall our very first meeting. We are mighty ninth graders in a Los Angeles junior high school, and we hit it off right from the start. He's almost a year older, which proves to become a bonus when we are close to driving age since we are both surfers. He's my ride to the beach as well as my friend!

How do we all make friends, anyway? I don't recall any class lessons on the subject or any guidance from my parents. We're just supposed to innately know what makes a friend, how to choose wisely, and how to be a good friend. Amazing! John's a good one. Lucky for me.

Being a surfer then is not the same as being one today. Similarly, being a surfer then is not the same as being a surfer in the 1950s or earlier. Pioneer surfers from Bob Simmons to Pat Curren and Greg Noll ride redwood and balsa wood boards, upwards of 100 pounds! Curren, Noll, and others eventually introduce the much lighter fiberglass boards in the late '50s.

Our surfboards in the 1960s, compared to those of today — though still made of fiberglass — are much longer and heavier, over nine and a half feet long and close to 35 pounds. The surf leash hasn't been invented, so our boards wash to shore when we fall off. Divers have thick, bulky wetsuits to wear for the cold ocean water, but surfers have not yet accepted wearing them in order to keep warm. The wetsuits, because of the thickness of the neoprene rubber, make it hard to paddle and stand up. They need to be lighter and more flexible. That will come. For now, John and I are too busy surfing all year long in just our trunks to worry about wetsuit design.

Then, being a real surfer meant a person had to be a strong swimmer. It helps to be more muscular since the board is large and heavy, and a stronger surfer can turn and maneuver the board more easily. Likewise, it helps to have a bit more meat on your bones in order to cope with the cold water.

Times have changed. Surfboards are much lighter and smaller today. With the advent of wetsuits and leashes, the smaller, thinner surfer can remain in the cold water and scoot all over the waves even more effectively than the larger guy.

Most of the places we surf north of Los Angeles have rocky shorelines, lots of kelp, and no lifeguard of any kind. Nobody is truly watching out for their pals in the water, either. We are competing for the best position for a wave, which usually arrives every five to ten minutes in a set of two, three, or four. Between sets, we might talk or horse around by squirting water at each other. Sometimes we just sit silently, deep in our own thoughts, pondering life, waiting…similar to going fishing.

On big days someone will yell, "Outside!" and we just try to survive the terror of paddling up the 12-foot vertical face of a feathering wave: getting the nose of the board punched by the cresting peak, feeling the agonizing sensation of plummeting backward, "over the falls", while still attempting to wrap our bodies around the board, having it wrenched from our grasp as we are smashed deep into the water and foam and bounced off the rocky bottom, robbed of any chance to breathe.

After all of that, you swim in for your board, which ends up getting dinged as it bounces off the rocks and boulders. We manage about an hour of surfing in the winter. Summer is much warmer and allows us to stay out longer. With ankles and shins dribbling blood mixed with sea water — thanks to the barnacles and jagged edges of those rocks walked across in order to retrieve a lost surfboard — and with surfer's hands so cold you need to ask for help to turn the key to unlock a car door, everything is just as it should be.

We gather on the beach around some burning wood or a black-smoke-belching tire. We warm up as we tell stories of our wave adventures. Sometimes, after one surfer finishes describing, in full detail, the critical take-off, how he had yelled, "Comin' down!" as he dropped in to warn others that he was on it and to keep out of the way, and the turn he made, and how he had barely made it through a huge section of breaking wave, well, then someone else who just happened to see the event, tells the true tale. Usually, it was half the size as in the first story and there was no recollection of any breaking section of wave. You could say surfers are like fishermen in this way, as well. We like to exaggerate.

However, there are times so rewarding, when someone DOES really see the great wave the guy catches and tells everyone in the circle all about it. It's wonderful just to gloat when this happens to you. There is always something funny to recall, too... the way somebody wipes out, the way their board sails into the air, the look on some nearby guy's face as he is almost run over... things like that.

Surfing is a tough sport in these early days, but it is certainly more rewarding than painful. Most of the time waves are smaller and those who are dedicated and who surf regularly make real progress and have many memorable experiences which keep us paddling back out as often as possible.

There is also a wonderful camaraderie as surfers meet at school or the beach, become friends, and hang out and go to the beach together. Car club members, hiking enthusiasts, musicians, dancers, and other sports participants may well know that same feeling of solidarity within their group. The big difference at this time is we surfers are pioneers since our equipment is in just its beginning phases – and there aren't that many of us in the water.

Another bonus is the surf culture exploding onto the pop-culture scene with the Beach Boys on radio and TV, sun-bleached blonde hair, Pendleton shirts, white Levi's jeans which stop just above the ankle, Jack Purcell tennis shoes, surfing vans and station wagons, perfect for your 10' board and a mattress in back for sleeping on the roadside at the beach...and the girls who come with all of this. Surf films produced by surfers play at your local high school auditorium. They are 16mm and the filmmaker is there to narrate over the background music and the cheer and chatter of the audience. Hollywood cashes in with its "Beach Blanket Bingo" movies. These fakes only exploit the surf scene and have nothing to do with the real culture of surfing and its heroes.

We do our schoolwork; some of us have part-time jobs; we spend time with our families. But sometimes, we just concern ourselves with how and when we can go surfing. My favorite surf beach is about an hour's drive from home.

There are some women surfing, too. I remember 25-year-old Annie surfing in her bikini all year long. She is good. She's very muscular. There is another girl, a friend of hers, whose surfboard we have to keep dodging all the time because she almost always falls off. I nickname her "Disaster." But, to her credit, she swims in for her board and just paddles back out to the waves. I remember Lil, wife to Ray, both probably in their forties, very old to us, who own a giant white van they use to sleep in overnight right on the Coast Highway. Lil surfs in the summer. She isn't very good, but because she doesn't catch many waves, she doesn't get in the way. Ray likes to take pictures. I wish I could find some of those now.

Because we often knee-paddle those large boards, we develop calcium deposits or "surf knots" on our knees and the tops of our feet. One foot tends to have a larger bump because you push off more with that one. Having surf knots is a badge of honor. For a while, some guys even avoid getting drafted for the Vietnam War because government doctors don't know how to classify these bumps, especially the ones on top of the foot! They think the bumps might be a birth defect or cancer. Before long, though, surf knots become common knowledge; the huge one on my right foot poses no problem as far as the Navy is concerned.

I tell you all of this so that you can better appreciate how great I feel when, now that we are in high school, John invites me to sleep over at his house the night before we are to go surfing. He drives now and owns a VW van. We can barely close our eyes because we're so excited! His alarm goes off in the dark around 4:30, we dress, grab some cereal and maybe a bag of chips and an apple for lunch, load the boards in, and are on the road before 5:00 A.M.

Within an hour, just before sunrise, we're pulling up to the rocky dirt clearing at our favorite beach. The air is probably in the low 50s and the water is in the mid- to upper-50s. Under the cover and privacy of a wrapped towel, in the manner surfers have perfected, we slide on our surfing trunks. Then we wax up our boards with Parowax (the same paraffin wax used for canning jam), and race down the dirt and stony hillside to the rock and sand beach below. It's a special honor to be the first one to paddle out on any given day. Welcome to surfing in my teens.

As I paddle out, I'm still smiling as I recall that night before at John's. I had arrived in time to join John and his family for dinner. John's older sister is there along with his mom and dad and little brother, David, who's in early elementary school. It's a warm summer's evening and even though the house has no air conditioning, the open windows make things manageable. The family loves their two pets, a dog and a cat, both now somewhere under the dinner table monitoring the floor for the inevitable vittles which may fall at any time.

The conversation ranges from brother-brother and brother-sister rivalries to what happened that day in the office. John's dad looks down under the table and notices the cat munching on a morsel of something and remarks, "Did I ever tell you the story about our cat, Smokey?"

Without pausing for a reply, he proceeds.

> One really hot August day a few years ago, we sat at this very table having lunch. Our cat was named Smokey. She was gray with white patches and paws. A very nice cat. Quite gentle. I remember her standing by that open window screen over there, just taking in the slight breeze, evidently trying to cool off. And I happened to

say something to everyone about how hot the cat must be with all her fur.

We finished lunch and everyone went off to find a place to beat the heat. But unknown to the rest of us, little David came up with a plan. He felt sorry for Smokey since she must be so hot. He picked her up and headed for the kitchen. No one was around. He opened up the freezer door and somehow pushed Smokey in and closed it! I guess his plan was to leave her there for a few minutes, let her cool off, and then open the door so she could jump out feeling much better!

Later that evening we gathered around the table for dinner. I think we had eaten and it was about time for dessert and I looked around and didn't see the cat. I asked, 'Has anyone seen Smokey?'

David jumped back, almost tipping over his chair. He yelled, 'Oh no!' and ran into the kitchen, swung open the freezer door, and again yelled, 'Oh no!'

We all leaped from our chairs and stampeded into the kitchen to see what was wrong. I peered in the freezer and there was Smokey, arms and legs outstretched, claws out, frozen solid! Her mouth was open as if she had been calling for help. It was a terrible, terrible sight.

I pulled her out and placed her poor frozen body on the dining room table. David was shrieking. 'I'm so sorry! I'm so sorry!' We were all in tears. I called the vet just to ask if there was anything we could do. I knew I'd heard of some fish who freeze in the winter and revive in the spring...some kind of suspended animation. And you know the stories of people who have fallen through the ice somewhere, drowned, and half an hour later were revived and were okay. I thought maybe…

It was nighttime, so we called an emergency vet. He told us there was not much chance Smokey could be revived, but we might try one thing. He asked if we had any kind of petroleum around like gasoline or anything. I told him we had a lawnmower and a gas can for it.

'Get an eyedropper. Fill it with gasoline. Now, is her mouth open at all? Otherwise, we have to try this through her nose.'

'Yes, her mouth is open.'

'Good, that's fortunate. Squeeze 3 eyedroppers-full of gas in her mouth and let it settle and work its way to her throat. See if there's any response of any kind.'

We thanked him and turned her frozen little body as it rested on the table so that we could manage the task. The first two dropper-fulls did nothing. We could see the gas sitting there in her little frozen open mouth, working its way down her throat, and we could smell it. When I put the third dropper of gas in her mouth, suddenly there was a sound, a vibration. Smokey started to shake! She trembled! She shuddered all over! She screamed!

Her legs shot out, she jumped up, and scrambled off the dining room table! Then she started to run in circles. She ran around and around this very dining room table three times and then she just plopped over!

The room is silent as John's dad finishes the story. I look at John.

I'm astounded! I mean, this is so amazing! But wait. I'm not clear. Is that the end of the story? What happens next? I can't understand it.

I look to John's dad and plead, "Was she dead?"

"No," is his answer. "She ran out of gas."

John and I have an excellent time surfing that next day. And I have a wonderful story to reflect upon while waiting for the next set of waves to come in.

Second Thoughts

※

Going back in time and seeing life through someone's eyes at the age you are now can reveal how different life was. But if you look closely, you can see, no matter what period in time they lived, how related people are in their need for friendship and a feeling of accomplishment. Sometimes we may not be willing to believe that older people understand our feelings and experiences, but recognizing these similarities reminds us of how valuable their insight can be. But, in contrast, sometimes we are willing to set aside our own understanding of what is possible simply because we put our trust into what someone we respect tells us. Ah, the challenges of life!

Dropping In Deeper

1. Can you picture a group of surfers standing around a burning tire at the beach? What do you think about that? Why do they do it? What makes this a positive experience?

2. Do you think there was much danger surfing in those days? Why or why not?

3. What do you think it was like being a girl surfing then? Explain.

4. Just as the author has to sometimes deal with big waves and fear while surfing, where in your life do you face fearful situations? How do you deal with them?

5. Did you find yourself believing the story of Smokey right until the end? Why or why not?

6. Describe a time in your life when you have known something is probably untrue, yet you have found yourself believing it, anyway.

7. What do you think makes a friend? How do you choose your friends?

8. Define what "innate" means as in "...to innately know..."

9. Where in your life do you find the kind of camaraderie, the feeling of friendship that the author shares with his surfing pals? If your answer is "I don't know," give an example of where you might.

10. Sketch the surfers telling stories while standing around a fire on the beach as your mind's eye see it, OR Smokey on that hot summer's day. Describe your picture with a caption.

Chapter 4: They're Out To Get Me - *Running Away & Talking To Someone When Worried Or Afraid*

I'm 9 years old, an immature nine-year-old at that, and my family of five is renting a two-story home in a residential neighborhood of downtown Los Angeles. I'm not quite settled. It seems I require some time to better understand my surroundings and the situations I find myself getting into. At this point, I just think "they're" out to get me, they meaning… everybody.

One and two-story houses, built in the '30s and '40s, line both sides of the street. Single skinny 80-foot-tall Mexican fan palm trees, a hundred feet apart, rise from the mowed strip of grass in front of each home. The trees seem to defy the laws of gravity and balance as they rustle and sway in the wind, looking like candles on a rectangular birthday cake. They're out to get me, too — tall palm trees are just perfect for snagging my kite the moment a gust of wind takes it in their direction.

About four doors down from the house we're renting lies a busy boulevard, honk-honk-honking its way through Los Angeles. I must be very careful crossing it, especially on my bike. I know those cars will get me if I don't watch out.

Only old people live nearby. There's no one to play with in the neighborhood except for my two younger brothers – and at ages five and seven, they're basically vegetables as far as I'm concerned. As the oldest, I'm always in trouble because Mom thinks I bully them or something. The middle brother howls like a siren whenever I touch him, starting low and then raising his pitch and volume. He's a master at it. Mom comes running and I'm always the one she blames. They're all out to get me. I'm having a tough year.

It's December. Christmas means Santa's coming soon. But there's a snag. I, of course, depend upon Mom and Dad for some of my presents. This means they have something over me for a month or so. This year I've asked them for a toy Sherman tank instead of a bunch of small stuff. It's a massive piece of Army-gray plastic and machinery; I mean, this thing is at least two feet long and a foot wide. It devours small hills, plastic army men, barriers devised of stones and sticks, oh, and at least eight batteries! I've been thinking about this tank for months. I can't wait for Christmas Day so I can set it loose on the vacant lot at the other end of our block.

But I'm in trouble. Big time. Unfortunately, on a whim one Saturday morning, I decide that a first-ever bike ride to a friend from school's house is the order of the day – it's about five miles to Steve's home. I don't tell anyone I'm going to do this, including him! It's a personal challenge and I take off just after breakfast. As I say, immature am I...and a bit impulsive.

Oh, I should mention that on that afternoon my whole family plans to head out to my school, about 45 minutes away by car, for a special school carnival.

I arrive at his Hollywood Hills house and surprise! He is home! We mess around for a while doing the kinds of things nine-year-olds do. Then I turn around and head back again over busy boulevards, residential streets, and hillsides. I must say all has gone really well on my four- or five-hour escapade to Steve's house. Returning home, I peddle up my block and see a police car in our driveway, sitting a bit cockeyed as if someone parked it in a hurry. I haven't considered they're out to get me, too!

Remember, no cellphones exist these days. There's a bit of pandemonium when, a little confused, I lay my bike on the lawn and walk through the front door. The police officer, standing just inside the house, spots me and the bike on the lawn and immediately recognizes the situation. He's seen it so many times before -- frantic parents having to cope with a ditzy kid. I can see it on his face. Mom and Dad, standing with him, at first appear joyful. Then in a quick moment, their expressions simultaneously morph into a quizzical and not-so-happy look. It's the kind of face, spritzed with embarrassment, a kid takes on when he first realizes someone stuck a "Kick me" sign on his back.

We do go to the carnival that afternoon. But in the evening, after returning home and settling down a bit, Mom delivers the message. Grounded. No bike riding. And I'm out one bitchin' tank I was supposed to get for Christmas! Horrors! Here we go again. Everyone's out to get me.

I'm really upset. That tank means everything to me. Now it's lost. So, being who I am, I decide to run away. That'll teach Mom and Dad a lesson.

It's raining that chilly winter night a bit before Christmas. Rain in Los Angeles is really special because it happens so rarely. Dinner is done. Mom's in the kitchen. I don't know where everyone else is, and I don't care. I put on my little windbreaker and, out of sight of everyone, just walk out the front door. I don't know where I'm headed. I just know everyone is out to get me.

The street's gutters are flowing with rain run-off. Los Angeles just isn't very accustomed to the stuff. I plop into the small torrent and slosh around in the streetlight-spotted darkness. I'm on my way.

About an hour into this, it's really getting cold. I'm feeling it. My jacket is soaked and sticking to my bare arms. I keep wiping away the wet hair mopping my eyes. Somehow, chilly rainwater trickles down my pants, over my butt, and down my legs. I'm kind of miserable and wondering what I should do next and then this brilliant idea comes to me. "I know, I'm gonna kick around in this water in the cold and dark and get pneumonia and die. Then they'll be sorry."

I love the idea. I'm ready. So, for another half-hour or so I wander aimlessly, through neighborhoods I don't know, along the boulevard as well, ready and accepting of my plight-to-be. Pneumonia, come get me!

Well, it doesn't. I get kind of numb from the cold and everything, but no pneumonia as far as I can tell. I keep expecting the cough to start, but no luck. So, gradually, and disappointedly, I start veering back towards the lights of home. Oh, I know there will be another police car in the driveway and another big hassle, but I just don't care. I just don't understand why pneumonia hasn't arrived.

Another few minutes meandering through wind and rain and

dark, and I arrive on my block. Mom and Dad must have called the police by now. My bet is they're as worried and sorry as Ralphie's parents in "A Christmas Story" when he returns home, blind, due to soap poisoning. I see my house ahead...but there's no police car. Fine. They must be out on patrol searching for me.

Up the steps and right to the front door I go to face my parents who must be feeling distraught and guilty by this time. They're probably sitting on the couch in the living room, my two younger brothers nearby, all just waiting for a phone call from the police. Sure, my brothers are probably more curious than worried, but that's okay. But Mom and Dad must be feeling wretched. They deserve it. They took away my tank.

I open the door and upon looking around I see... no one! I'm sopping wet. Water is dripping off me onto the carpet like there is a busted toilet upstairs and it's leaking from the ceiling. So, I decide to slam the door shut, really hard and loudly! Bam! I don't understand where everyone is! Then Mom comes out from the kitchen, peeks around the doorway, looks at me with a confused tilt of the head, and asks, "Peter, did you go outside? I thought you were upstairs doing your homework."

What? Nobody even cares enough to notice whether I'm even home? All this cold and wet and wandering misery I've gone through, and no one even bothers to think about me or what's happened?

You know, Life's like that. You can't assume what will happen or predict what's ahead for you.

Nothing much comes from this escapade. As far as my parents are concerned, I have been outside playing in the oh-so-rare rain for a few minutes. No big deal.

I never tell anyone what really happened that day. Why bother?

They're all just out to get me, anyway.

Oh, Christmas morning...somehow, I get the tank after all.

But I don't get pneumonia.

Second Thoughts

※

We all have times when it seems everything and everyone is against us. Sometimes it's like a dark cloud just hanging over our head. Sometimes it's just that we're in a bad mood and nothing seems right. Sometimes we REALLY DO have excellent reasons for feeling low. But it's what we do about it that matters. This little guy doesn't have the maturity to reach out and talk to anyone about how he feels. Do we just sit and stew and get angry like he does? Do we run away to try to make everybody feel sorry? These aren't good solutions. You're old enough. Find someone you can talk to about your feelings. It may be a best friend, a brother or sister, or an adult like a teacher or counselor at school. Sometimes it helps to write about your feelings and then share them with that person. But don't keep everything inside of you. Work through it and you'll find you can make the clouds go away and the sun shine bright again! Honest!

Dropping In Deeper

1. Give an example of why the author feels, "They're out to get me!"

2. Describe a time when you felt people were being unfair and out to get you, or that life was unfair and making things harder for you.

3. Why are the author's parents so upset with him when he returns from his bike trip?

4. This is a young boy's story. Do you think girls have some of the same thoughts and feelings? Explain.

5. What is the definition of "frantic" as in "...frantic parents..."? Use it in a sentence.

6. What is a better way the author's parents could handle the situation besides threatening to take away his precious tank?

7. Sketch the author wandering through the rain as your mind's eye sees it OR what he sees when he arrives home after the bike ride. Describe your picture with a caption.

8. Describe a time when you behaved in an impulsive way and did something without thinking of the effect it will have upon

others.

9. Why do you think the author's parents give him the tank at the end of the story?

10. Have you ever run away, or wanted to? Why? What was going on?

11. At one point, as the author sloshes through the gutters full of rainwater, he just wants to be gone. Have you ever felt that way? Somewhere along the way most of us do. If so, what caused you to feel so down? How did you get over it?

12. What is a lesson you learn from this story? At the end does it seem the author learns his lesson?

Chapter 5: Bridging The Gap - *Taking Risks & Valuing Common Sense*

My first glimpse of her is in my junior college Sociology I class - long brown hair, cinnamon-brown eyes, a light complexion that tans so well in the summer mountain sun. Her teeth are sugar cube white. Her voice seems a little shrill at times, but those times become less frequent. She's truly lovely.

I'm a face guy, and for me, I couldn't ask for more. She has the figure that commands a 22-year-old guy's attention. After a couple of years in the Navy, I'm ready for college and the fringe benefits it offers.

These are the days when you can go to class barefoot, bring your dog, and smoke if that's what you do. Your professor may be smoking a pipe!

Mr. Yacov is our professor. You can tell he is sincere and totally dedicated to even the driest statistics part of his sociology lectures. He wants to help the World be a better place. He tends to be a bit dull and unmoving. It's a 1:00 pm class, and that's my nap time. About halfway through his lecture, I find myself struggling to keep awake. I solve this problem by becoming a front-row regular – sitting close to the "action" just as much to keep awake as to garner anything from his presentations.

I wait until I'm getting sleepy, which is about the same time you can see white spittle forming at the corners of his mouth. Mr. Yacov sprays a bit when he lectures - you just get used to it sitting up front. I raise my hand to ask a question. I know he will allow almost anything even remotely related to his topic. He answers, we may or may not have an exchange of ideas, but at least this sidetracks him from his prepared lecture and adds some variety to the session. It also reawakens me. Now I'm reinvigorated until the blessed bell!

Apparently, this helps him keep awake as well! Some twenty years later I run into him at Home Depot. I say, "Hi Mr. Yacov! I was a student of yours years ago."

When I tell him my name he excitedly recalls, "I remember you! You are the student who always asked those great questions! You helped keep my class interesting!" Years later, as a classroom teacher myself, I keep this conversation close to my heart. Mr. Yacov is an inspiration…of sorts.

But back to her. She sits somewhere toward the rear of the classroom. I soon discover she is yet another technique to help me stay awake, and now this is one class I never skip for the beach! I find myself excited about attending Mr. Yacov's 1:00 p.m. Sociology I class on Mondays, Wednesdays, and Fridays.

Oh, and I soon move my seat a bit farther to the back of the class next to her. I know I won't be getting sleepy anymore.

At this point in time, I surf and study and work some. I don't know where I'm going but I'm on my way! This young woman serves up the spice missing from my life, only she doesn't know it. In time I work up the gumption to talk to her. We spend time together, leave notes on each other's car windows, and share poems we've both read and written. I sing to her, we sing together, and we fall in love. She is my first true love.

She works part of the summer as a counselor at a mountain camp just south of the Sierras and helps get me hired as a counselor, so our adventures continue. While the campers attend the evening campfire session, the two of us go for a mischievous moonlight swim in the camp pool. It makes that "What I Did on Summer Vacation" composition so much more fun to write!

Later that summer we raise the stakes and go camping as a couple with her friends at a lake near Yosemite. This is just another memory, but it inserts its way into this story for another reason.

A 30' high bridge straddles a tributary to the lake. There should be a sign on it reading, "Go On. Leap!" It just calls to you! A small group of us make the jump a few times. After one of my jumps, while treading water, I get curious. I ask myself, "How deep do you suppose this murky water is?" It doesn't look all that impressive. It's summer, so there's not much flow feeding the lake, and the bridge's pilings appear to be set just a few feet below the surface. I wonder if there might be a shallow spot with rocks or something dangerous to a jumper, or if the bottom is just mushy mud.

Instead of climbing up the embankment for another attempt

at hurtling — or hurting — myself, I decide to explore and find out how deep this tributary stream goes. I'm just beyond where everyone lands. The warm summer water and hot sun inspire me. I take a couple of deep breaths, close my eyes to keep out the muddiness and start the feet-first descent.

I propel myself downward by repeatedly lifting upward with both hands cupped. At first, I must force my way deeper, my toes constantly pointed down waiting for that first touch of the unknown bottom which beckons me. It's a lot of work. In a very short time, I am surprised to feel the water turning chilly. I am achieving depth! Though this is a tributary feeding into the lake just 40 yards away, the water seems to just sort of settle there. Like I thought — no apparent flow.

While I'm delving to find rock bottom, let's stop for a moment to consider what we are taught in school. Let's ponder all the hours of our lives we spend trying to conquer algebra, grammar, and the science of cell mitosis. But does anyone teach us about how to be in a relationship, how to make a friend, how to be a good friend, good manners, or practical skills (read: survival)? Not usually.

Not really. We don't learn these subjects in school unless we are fortunate enough to have a great English teacher who guides us to the lessons of life provided in literature. And, even then, the writer's intended message tends to be more of the focus rather than those essential side lessons we might discover. This is just something for you to ponder.

Now, back to the descent. My toes stretch out, ready to touch the bottom and push off. My eyes remain closed. I continue the incessant upward motion of my arms. Up to this point, I've had to push hard because my body seems buoyant in the water. But now, I'm travelin'! I'm heading down!

After maybe10 seconds of all this movement, with the water gradually cooling and my eyelids perceiving darker surroundings...I realize something. There is still no squishy bottom, and I DON'T HAVE TO PUSH UPWARD TO DESCEND ANYMORE! I feel more like a rock headed to the bottom – wherever that is. I can feel the water seeming to flow upward. My ears are especially sensitive to a change in pressure, which means I'm going down rapidly! It's a situation similar to a frog in a pot of gradually heating water. So, the story goes, the frog in the pot never quite figures out in time what's going on and instead of hopping out, he gets too comfortable and gradually nods off to become dinner. I'm on my way to oblivion, to the end of me!

I'm a college kid. I'm smart. I graduated from a good high school. Yet I am unable to recall any lessons about water density and pressure and what happens to the buoyancy of a body containing air as it drops into the depths - at least not at this moment. The fact is that the air compresses, reducing buoyancy as water pressure or depth increases. What is happening to me now is the reverse of what happens to a helium-filled weather balloon as it rises in the atmosphere and expands as the higher-altitude air pressure diminishes. I've gone deep enough to lose any ability to float. I'm getting compressed. I'm hurtling myself to the bottom.

I'm on the verge of joining that frog, or to switch metaphors, getting my goose cooked!

Somehow, I become aware of all of this and work to reverse my course. I claw and kick for everyone who has ever loved me, for every wave I ever hope to ride, and for every person who considers me their friend – maybe even a little for myself! I'm running out of breath. My eyes, now wide open and unblinking like a zombie, ignore that murky water as they search for any sign of light, of life, in order to be certain I am approaching the surface.

Yes, I have abandoned the all-essential quest to discover the bottom and whether it's squishy or rock-laden. It just doesn't seem that important anymore!

I barely make it, come up floundering and coughing, and... nobody notices! My girlfriend has just climbed up the hillside to the bridge again and clearly, I've been off her to-do list for the last couple of minutes.

I straggle up onto the bridge. There's a small group about to take the leap again, she among them. Up pulls Johnny Law in his black and white police car. "There's no jumping off the bridge!" he yells out the car window as one guy perches on the concrete railing, turning to look at the cop like a deer caught in the headlights of a car. The lawman slowly, in practiced fashion, pushes the car door open and saunters up to the group. The would-be diver steps down off the bridge railing to the adjacent sidewalk.

"In the last month, we've had two of you kids drown jumping off this very bridge."

I may still be all wet from my exploration session a few minutes prior, but I'm no longer "wet behind the ears," an old expression meaning naive. No, now I understand completely. I realize HOW THOSE KIDS PROBABLY DROWNED...as well as the so-many-others I've heard about over the years who jumped off a bridge, pier, or cliff. THEY DOVE TOO DEEP...LOST BUOYANCY...AND COULD NOT FIND THEIR WAY TO THE SURFACE IN TIME. I just experienced that with, fortunately, a happier ending.

Just one lesson in school about the dynamics of a body's density in water, buoyancy, and diving might have saved their lives. But they died, their heads instead weighted down with the quadratic equations of algebra, the meaning of a preface or the year of the Mongolian invasion. For me, this lesson about the buoyancy of a body as it descends in water is essential; it has certainly etched its way into my life and memories and is now part of my wisdom.

The grilled chicken we enjoy later that evening tastes extra special...perhaps a little bit like frogs' legs...

Second Thoughts

※

There are times we take risks for a good reason, and there are times we are just being foolish. Wisdom helps us recognize how to avoid putting ourselves in harm's way, especially because there are not always signs posted in public places to help us with this challenge – or we just ignore them. We can learn some lessons in life, lessons in survival, and lessons about relationships through literature, and not actually have to experience every downfall and mistake. When someone – like a teacher, a parent, or myself — tells a tale, the reader can live life and make discoveries through those written experiences. Common sense will always be the basis for most of these lessons. Learn to listen to them. Treasure those you find useful and make them yours.

Dropping In Deeper

1. If the author were in his 30s or 40s, would he still be as likely to jump? Why or why not?

2. If you are with a group of friends considering jumping off a bridge, pier, or cliff, and you feel uncomfortable about it and you really don't want to jump, how can you handle the situation?

3. What connection can you make to this story and any TV news or events in your life?

4. Describe a time when you decided not to do something dangerous or foolish.

5. Skateboarding in the street in traffic is not safe. Yet we have all seen someone do this. Why would you suppose they do it?

6. Describe a time when, as a friend or concerned person, you warned someone that what they were doing was not safe.

7. Sketch the guy who is stopped as he is about to jump off the bridge as your mind's eye sees it OR the bridge as the author sees it looking up from the water. Describe your picture with a caption.

8. Is it good or not-so-good that Mr. Yacov remembers the

author for making his class more interesting? Why?

9. What is the meaning of "incessant" as in "...I continue the incessant upward motion of my arms..."? Use it in a sentence.

Chapter 6: Bodies Surfing

– *Developing Self-Confidence With Someone You Find Attractive*

A coastal late afternoon in June dawns the customary San Diego Gloom, the pesky gray-sky marine layer that hangs over the beach, blocking any sunlight and making the air much chillier than it should be. But if you look inland, you can see the sunshine, warm on the tan green hills a mile or two in the distance – just out of reach. It's a tad frustrating to feel so cold while others not that far away are donning sunglasses.

I'm 21, have served my time in Nixon's Vietnam War, and now attend college. But it's summer, so I'm at the beach. Of course, if it were fall or winter, I'd still be at the beach. After all, I'm 21 going on 19! And I'm a surfer. I'm catching up on the two years I have been away in the Navy.

The boulders of the Ocean Beach jetty stand guard just about 100 feet up the shoreline from where I'm standing. They pit themselves against the constantly surging water, waves, and spray as they help protect the beach sand from the currents, while providing, on the other side, a throughway for ocean-going vessels.

It's a lonely feeling to look out on this day. I can't spot anybody, not even a lifeguard, as wearing only swim trunks I wade out 25 yards into the surf. With each step the sandy bottom oozes just a bit between my toes. The sullen skies and foreboding spray cause me to hope I am never reincarnated into one of those gray, cold, boulder soldiers.

Allow me to provide a brief oceanography lesson here. You can better appreciate the goosebumps!

The ocean remains a bit chilly, maybe 63 degrees, like it's trying to fight off the warming effect of the Southern California Bight. This is a current that recirculates counterclockwise between Point Conception and San Diego, allowing the summer sun to raise its temperature maybe 5 degrees or more. Picture a stream where some rocks jut out and leaves swirl around in the water within the rocks. Just beyond, the stream flows steadily. That swirling water with leaves in tow is the Bight.

Yet just a few more miles out to sea, an undisturbed current runs from north to south - the colder California Current. It comes back to the shoreline a few miles farther south in Baja, making the Mexican waters colder than those to the north in San Diego!

The slate-colored sea and mushy afternoon waves still appeal to me for bodysurfing. I'm wading out into waist-high water where I can push off with my feet as I swim with the surge of a wave, catch it, and ride it in with only my head exposed. Sometimes I can get all the way to the shore where it's only six inches deep.

The only sign of summer is that I'm in the water just trunkin' it. My skin, with all its goosebumps, looks more like 30 grit sandpaper, but I keep jumping into waves and riding them as far as I can until my nose drags on the sand. I charge back out into the surf – heating myself up like my own California Bight. It's a good day.

Then comes the unexpected. No, not the sun popping out making the water a beautiful popsicle blue. No, not even the Wave of the Day, a wave so huge it carves its way into my memory banks forever. No, it's a different kind of surprise. Just as I'm about to push off with my feet and swim hard for another wave, in the chest-high surf appears, like a mermaid, a lovely bikini-clad girl. not ten feet from where I'm standing in the water!

From deep within some little convolution of my brain, possibly a primordial directive going back to the beginning of man, arises the mantra known to many a young lad, "Don't look at her!"

But for God's sake, here we are, no one else is in the water for half a mile, and this attractive woman has chosen to put herself 10 feet away! Why not look at her and make eye contact!? Instead, I'm faithful to my immediate instinct.

Without uttering a word or catching another glimpse, I grab the next wave. So does she!

When I bodysurf, my eyes stay closed for the first part of the ride. It's silly but has something to do with not getting saltwater in them. Eventually, you must look at where you're headed somewhere down the way, but for that moment, I'm sightless.

As I chug along in the foam, I'm thinking about this whole mystical situation: a girl, a woman really, about my age, is in the surf with me. I hope she's still…AND THEN…

I don't know if I can even describe it! Across those goosebumps on my chest and legs momentarily passes the sensation of a warm, wet chamois – I know this isn't the most attractive descriptor, but it's how it feels! It's certainly better than comparing it to Jonah's sensations as he's swallowed by the whale, sliding down in the slippery blackness of the whale's throat!

As I said, it's momentary. Is it a small clump of seaweed? Have I bumped up against a large jellyfish? Nah, it is something good. Very good. It is she, as her lotion-slicked, uncovered skin finds a way to greet mine in the turbulence of white froth and natural desire.

I open my eyes, of course, but in the foam and frolic of water and waves, there is nothing to see. She is nowhere.

I have found the cure for goosebumps!

I stand up in the shin-deep remnants of waves now past their prime and turn my head in time to see her, fanny facing me, gracefully wading again back into the surf.

Of course, I follow. Of course! But not too closely.

The next 15 minutes may well be the most spontaneous, yet sensual, of my life. We catch at least five waves together, each time her thigh, her chest, or her bare stomach momentarily skimming across my bare chest and legs and back. Never a word is spoken. Never do my eyes open in the foam. Never do our eyes meet.

At this point, I start to ponder something to say. It's evident it will be up to me.

Maybe I could mention something clever about a supposed piece of seaweed I see hanging from the back of her bikini bottom. Or I could casually tell her how great it is to have a buddy to bodysurf with. I know. I'll smile and say, "Your wet hair all wound around that way looks like a delicious cinnamon roll!"

I charge back out into the surf, all ready with my clever quip as soon as she comes up beside me again. I look out to the horizon and spot a fair-sized wave on its way from the end of the jetty. I'm all set. I turn towards her, ready to utter those words, which, who knows, could lead to us tossing out the "strange" in "strangers."

She isn't there! She's gone! Only those lonely gray cold soldiers remain in sight. I stand dumbfounded in the waist-deep water, like the cartoon Wylie Coyote staring at where the Roadrunner was just a second before. I can't believe it! Bam! That wave wallops me on the side of the head!

When I surface in the churning ocean, as the saltwater atop my head pours over my eyes, blinking open like the windshield getting the rinse cycle at the car wash, the shoreline comes into sight. Trudging away, down the beach, towel around her shoulders instead of my arm, and beach sack in hand, wanders my mermaid.

She never even looks back over her shoulder.

For if she had, I would have pursued her and said those words I know would have changed our encounter into a relationship.

But she didn't.

I wish she would have.

Second Thoughts

※

In 1962 Eddie Hodges explains it all in a song called "(Girls, Girls, Girls) Made to Love". These days you can find it on YouTube. I wish I had listened to him back then. And of course, the same kind of song could be sung about boys. How often have you wished a person you don't know, but whom you find attractive, would just come up to you and say, "Hello!"? We often put the responsibility for opening the conversation and getting acquainted with the other person.

You may be bashful. But just remember, a lot of people have the same needs as you. Sometimes they need your help to "get started." Keep that in mind for the next time and say, "Hello!"

Dropping In Deeper

1. What are the "gray cold boulder soldiers" in the story?

2. What is a chamois? If you haven't ever used one, find out how one feels when it's dry. Then discover what one feels like when it's soaking wet.

3. Do you think the girl is bodysurfing near the author on purpose? Why or why not?

4. Sketch the ocean and jetty as your mind's eye sees it OR the view from the water looking inland. Describe your picture with a caption.

5. What is the definition of "primordial" as in "...possibly a primordial directive going back to the beginning of man..." ? Also, a "convolution" would be where in your body?

6. What do you feel is the reason the author doesn't say anything to the girl? Is it a good reason? Why or why not?

7. When have you faced a situation where you didn't feel confident enough to say or do something? Did you feel regret afterward? Why or why not?

8. Does the author seem to have learned any kind of lesson at the

end of the story? What lesson do you learn?

Chapter 7: The Incredible Shrinking Boy - *Coping With Fright & The Importance Of Asking For Help*

Standing on the bow of a small yacht on a sunny day as it sits idle just off the coast, he notices a strange small sparkly silver cloud drifting in towards him close to the water. His wife has headed below to the cabin to make sandwiches. In moments the cloud surrounds him like fog, and soon floats away. But something has happened. His wife returns with lunch and notices queer little sparkles all over his chest and arms. They won't come off.

The fellow and his wife return home. Life seems normal until a couple of weeks later, as he's putting on his long-sleeve dress shirt, he realizes the sleeves are hanging down past the end of his hands! Soon he and his wife realize he's actually shrinking! Doctors can't help. Eventually, he's living inside a dollhouse, almost gets killed by the house cat as it chases him under the closed cellar door, and he climbs down a stair step only to have a house spider almost turn him into a cocoon. He uses a dropped sewing needle to defend himself. In the end of the story, he climbs through a tiny square of the basement screen and works his way down to the backyard, his last words being, "And I'm still shrinking."

The mysterious cloud turns out to be a radioactive leftover of atmospheric nuclear test explosions. In the 1950s, the release date of the movie from which this scene originates, aboveground atomic bomb tests were a common occurrence in Nevada, the South Pacific, and Russia.

In those days and in those kinds of movies, man-made radioactivity from atom bombs and atomic research facilities gets blamed for creating everything from giant dinosaurs stirred up from the ocean bottom which attack Tokyo, London, and New York, to radioactive slime slithering onto ships and land, turning people into foam. These are imaginative days for moviemakers, and the audience just begs to be frightened by the unknown.

As a seven-year-old having gone to the movies to watch this, I can't understand the notion that radioactivity can make someone shrink. And I certainly can't discern that the whole premise is ridiculous. I just see that somehow this guy, with strange sparkles on his chest, is getting smaller and smaller. I don't ever forget this.

I take in "The Incredible Shrinking Man" with my five-year-old brother at the matinee we routinely walk to every Saturday afternoon. When I say, "routinely", I mean I don't even bother to look up at the marquis to see what is playing. We just pay our quarter each to get a ticket, walk in and buy our popcorn and candy bar, and sit down in the auditorium. He can't understand much of anything except the Woody Woodpecker cartoon that shows just before the movie starts. Everyone always cheers when the curtains part and the cartoon appears. The last of our routine is to go home, have dinner, and go to bed. And even though this movie is scary, I'm fine. I don't even get to have a nightmare from it! It's just another movie.

Two years later, on a very warm summer evening, my now seven-year-old brother and I head back to our shared bedroom after having finished our homework and dinner. We don't have any air conditioning, but that's okay. I put on my pajamas and notice something. It seems my sleeves hang down past the tips of my fingers! What? I don't remember this ever happening! I flashback to that movie from years prior, "The Incredible Shrinking Man". It seems like I just saw it. I begin to wonder.

Nine-year-olds are a lot of fun. They're so aware of so much that is going on around them. They understand some of the news on TV, know how to turn to page 147 minus 6 (page 141) in their literature book when the teacher puts it that way, and are discovering puppy love – and I'm not talking about puppies!

I'm one of those nine-year-olds. I know a little about a little. It's bedtime, but I'm really worried now. I can't sleep. My little brother in the bed beside mine is already deep into his dream session. I'm wondering if I could somehow be headed the same way as that poor fellow in the movie! I go into the bathroom, flip the switch and look at myself in the mirror and there they are! In the bright light, I can see these really tiny sparkles on my chest near my neck! What are they? I don't remember having ever seen anything like this!

I do the only thing my little brain can conjure up. With ruler and pencil in hand, bright bathroom light a-shining, I back up against the wallpaper, place that ruler as flat over the top of my head as I can, and draw a line to mark my height at that moment. I figure I can check it later and see if anything has changed.

Uneasily I flip off the light (must save electricity like Dad says) and head back to bed. After a long while of trying to sleep (maybe 20 minutes), I jump up, flip on the light, back up against the wall again, place the ruler on top of my head, measure again...creating a new pencil line on the wallpaper. Oh man...it comes out below the first one! Oh man!

Click the light switch. Back into bed I go. Try to sleep. No idea of how long I lie there...up again, light on, measure - oh man, it comes out below the second one! No doubt. I'm shrinking!

"What are these tears all about?" I ask myself. I'm almost in a panic. I go through the same light routine and settle under the covers again. I don't know how I make it through the night. I keep thinking of that spider almost killing the shrinking guy. I wonder if I can make it 'til morning before being crushed by my blanket since it will be so giant for me by then. I keep envisioning him climbing through that screen and wandering deep into the garden dirt, like being in a boulder-filled area of a vast desert. How do you survive? How do you avoid getting eaten by an ant or spider? What do roly-poly bugs eat? Would they eat little me? What am I going to do? The tears are really streaming now...

My eyes open to a clear-sky new day! There's something about sunlight in the morning which changes things and makes everything okay. You know the feeling? My brother stirs. He calls out, "Hey!" I look around and I'm not crushed to death under the blanket as I had feared. My head still fits the pillow. I yell back, "Hey!"

Everything is kind of foggy. Did I really go through that torturous night, or did I just dream it? I jump out of bed and make it first to the bathroom. My brother is already hassling me outside the door yelling, "I gotta go! I gotta go!" The light is still burning. Did I mess up and leave it on? A look at the bathroom wall tells me everything. There are those wiggly lines scratched in pencil in the middle of the night.

The ultimate test is still to be taken. I rush over to the chair where my blue jeans lie. I slide in each leg with an apprehensive sigh. I pull the pants up, zip them tight...ah, perfect fit! They're just a bit above my ankle bone so there's plenty of sock showing. Just like I like it! Off I go, barging into the bathroom to use the mirror. The heck with my little brother's privacy. This is important!

No sparkles. They're gone! Whew! I settle down to a beautiful day of sunshine and normalcy. It comes to me later in the day that the sparkles were merely little beads of sweat reflecting the bathroom light. It was a warm night, indeed.

But that's not quite the end of the story.

A few months go by and I'm at the movies again, this time with a friend. I feel older now and a lot wiser than I used to be. What's the movie? "The Blob." It's about some Jell-O-like stuff that rolls its way out of a cracked-open meteorite and starts absorbing people. It can ooze under furniture and through the vent on a closed door. And it keeps getting LARGER!

Oh man! It's the middle of the night again. Our bedroom is so dark! I need to go to the bathroom. But if I climb out from under the covers, I know that Blob lying under the bed is going to absorb me! Gotta go! No. Gotta wait...for that morning sun.

Second Thoughts

※

Sometimes, even though there are people around us, we can feel very alone. Part of living is to be frightened from time to time. Being afraid, even being worried, is normal...for a while. It can make life interesting and a challenge. But if this fear or worry doesn't get settled, doesn't get worked out in some way, it can grow into a "Blob" of its own, absorbing all the joy you know in your life. Don't let that "Blob" exist. If you find you can't take care of that fear (or) that worry in short order, you need to talk about it with someone you trust and who has the wisdom to give you good advice. This might NOT be your best friend who might be as young and uninformed as you! It might be a parent or other adult family member or friend, a teacher, a counselor, or a religious leader. Keep the "Blob" out of your life...forever.

Dropping In Deeper

1. What were those sparkles on the author's neck and chest? Why was he so worried about them?

2. Why do you think the author doesn't wake up his little brother and tell him about the shrinking? Would you? Is it a bad idea to go to scary movies like these? Why or why not?

3. Why do you think the author keeps getting smaller measurements with the ruler?

4. What does the word "apprehensive" mean as in "...slide in each leg with an apprensive sigh..."? Then use your own word for "apprehensive" in a new sentence.

5. If you were a girl in this story, who would be the first person you would tell about this fear of shrinking? Why?

6. When have you found that when morning comes, things get better?

7. Sketch the two brothers walking up the street to the movie theater as your mind's eye sees it OR sketch the author measuring himself on the bathroom wall. Describe your picture with a caption.

8. When you're worried about something, when something is really bothering you, it's important to tell someone about it. Don't keep it in. Don't keep it a secret. If this story were yours, who would you have chosen to tell about the shrinking? When? Why would it be that person?

9. When have you faced a scary time? How did you manage to work it out?

10. What's the name of the scariest movie you have ever seen? What made it so scary for you?

Chapter 8: George –
Appreciating Worthiness In Others

S ome look back at their high school years as a "walk down memory lane," remembering new friends, adventures, and loves. After all, there is no other time in life, until retirement if you're lucky, when a person might realize so many budding abilities while coping with so few demands. High school, and maybe later in life during retirement, are times that leave open the opportunity to devote precious moments to new hobbies, skills, friendships, learning a musical instrument, a new language, a craft, a sport, writing, understanding politics, and more. For many, high school is a time ripe with exploration into the surrounding World. Remember this. This is a lesson in itself.

Yet for others, high school represents the worst years of their lives. There are social and emotional adjustments to make, feelings that they're not being accepted, family crises, academic concerns, and the unexpected broken heart or two. Being skilled at anything, having that ability to feel successful at something, seems to have escaped and there is envy of others who seem to revel in each day.

One essential person in my high school years is George. He helps make high school a great time by contributing to some of my best moments. He adds excitement and what will be rich memories, and he doesn't even know it! Strangely, we are more acquaintances than friends, and it's only when I look back upon our times together that I realize this.

I first meet George when I'm in 7th grade. He doesn't go to my school, but on weekends I get to play football with him and a few of the guys in the neighborhood on Lyle's front lawn. We pass, kick, and run the football where only a sidewalk and a patch of separate grass separate us from the boulevard. Yet the football never bounces into the traffic. Amazing!

George lives down the block from me in a colonial-style home, two stories tall, white, with two huge pillars guarding the front entrance. He's older than I am, and in the years to follow he gets his license and a car and offers us rides to the beach to go surfing. As we wander into our high school years, the relationship continues but never turns into the "lifelong friends" kind.

I can't say in which of the two realms he would place himself today: having loved or hated high school. But I can share the limited knowledge I have of his high school world. George can't be described in a word such as "average" or "gifted." He's "unique."

For instance, as the guys tell it, he has applied to the same military school they attend, but he cannot pass the entrance exam. He is a really nice guy who just doesn't appear to be as smart as the others.

I get to witness a couple of instances that reinforce this idea of his lack of savvy, his lack of ability to understand what is happening around him.

George gets a classic white '60 Ford T Bird from his dad. If you've ever seen the movie "American Graffiti," then you've seen a very young Suzanne Somers in a car similar to George's, except his has a back seat. Having a license and a car before the rest of us, he takes three of us along for the 50-mile journey to County Line Beach to surf. We chip in for gas. I can still see his beautiful sports car with four heavy 10' longboards strapped on a surf rack on top.

During the ride, we talk. One conversation takes place as we are headed home from surfing. We are driving south on the Coast Highway, coming down the hill into the city of Malibu, easily going 70 mph. George has a habit of turning to look at who he's talking to in the back seat – while he's driving!

"Pete, did you see that wave I caught off the point just before we came in?" Then he looks forward again at the road. Johnny and I in the backseat can see the traffic ahead just fine, as can Rick sitting shotgun.

He turns to us again. "It was really a great wave, and I rode it all the way in!" Meanwhile, up ahead maybe three blocks in our same lane, a Chevy station wagon has its left turn signal on and has stopped to make a turn into the gas station at the bottom of the hill.

All three of us see it, but not George. We are coming up fast on the wagon. The problem is that when George quits speaking and turns to face traffic again, HE KEEPS GOING 70! For whatever reason, he just doesn't notice that a car is stopped less than 100 yards ahead!

"George. George! GEORGE LOOK OUT!" we scream, almost in unison. It is then that everything registers, he spots the stopped vehicle, left blinker still pulsing, and hits the brakes as we careen in a four-wheel slide well past where the station wagon… had been. Evidently, the guy spots us, or hears our screeching tires, pounds down on the gas pedal, and clears out. He can fill up elsewhere.

Meanwhile, the poor surf rack can't take the stress and it lets go just as we finish our burned rubber slide. All four boards and the rack bounce off that gorgeous white hood, scraping it as they slam into the ground. When all the dust and smoke clear, there we are, in the middle of the Coast Highway in Malibu, with a broken-apart rack and two smashed surfboards on the ground in front of us. Johnny's and mine rest on top of the pile, undamaged.

"You idiot! You clod! What were you thinking?!" I don't remember who is the loudest or how many curse words are uttered, but I do know that to be the gist of the conversation for the next few minutes.

George just hangs his head. After we reattach the rack and load up all the boards, he doesn't have much to say. And he doesn't turn his head to speak to us…all the way home.

Ah, but there's more.

As the four of us are returning home from surfing on another day, this time driving east through the winding Malibu Canyon Road, and speeding right along with George at the wheel, it happens again.

Not the four-wheel slide maneuver, but something just as "special."

Johnny claims, "That wave I caught in the middle of the kelp was wild! I could hardly paddle into it. My fin kept getting stuck in kelp!" as we hastily cruise along the winding two-lane canyon road. He just finishes saying that when suddenly our faces all turn bright red! It is eerie, almost like a scene from a science fiction movie! I look at Johnny, who already has red hair, and he has turned this brilliant red color, flaming hair included. Everyone else has changed color, too, including George.

We look behind us through the rear window. It's the sheriff!

Yup, riding right on our bumper is a black-and-white (what we call a cop car in Southern California), bright red lights on, shinin' right through George's rear window and reflecting off his rearview mirrors onto our faces. It feels like the inside of the car must be heating up at least 10 degrees. We all look like barbecued chicken sitting under the red heating lamp at the grocery store.

But George just keeps on driving as if nothing is going on! This continues for about a minute. Finally, I say, "George. Hey George! There's a cop behind you!"

"I know. Do you think he wants me to pull over?"

"Yes, George."

We end our surf day not only with a ticket for speeding but with a pissed-off cop who's fairly upset at how long George continues driving before stopping. As for us, we lose a day of wave memories. After all that, who could possibly recall now what went on at the beach?

There is, however, another side to George. It is the end of another fun day surfing County Line. There's lots of good surf to remember. George is at the wheel, driving south on the

Pacific Coast Highway where it skims the beach just north of that Malibu hill. It's just the two of us this time, so I'm riding shotgun.

As we drive along the highway, parallel to the beach, we see small waves breaking on the sand. Each one builds and collapses all at once rather than with any form. By that I mean the waves don't fold over in a way a surfer could ride (if they were larger) going left or right in blue water ahead of white water. These are the kind of waves a painter portrays – just some green and blue and some white foam mixed in here and there. The waves just break all at once.

George looks over his shoulder as he observes the waves to his right and he poses this question to me, "As a surfer, can you ever look at a wave anywhere without considering whether it's rideable?"

This is not something that has ever occurred to me. It is a profound question, as is the moment. I suddenly realize I will never again be able to view waves without judging and evaluating them from a surfer's view. It doesn't matter if they are waves at Malibu or Lake Superior. Similarly, a skier doesn't look at a mountain covered with snow without weighing how the downhill would be. A skateboarder looks at a winding and sloping street and wonders about how much fun it would be to ride. When we learn a special skill, we develop a new perspective that will affect how we interact with our World from then on.

One might consider this a refinement in appreciation acquired through experience, that is, appreciating something once you've had more opportunities to interact with it. But it may also be the result of a loss of the innocence of just not being aware. Not knowing about something, being ignorant – which is not the same as being stupid – often means life is less complex and we find fewer things that concern us.

So, here's "Not-So-Smart George" with his observation about evaluating waves. Clearly, I'm lacking in awareness. He has abilities that we, as his friends, have overlooked. I wish I could say to him now, "Thank you, George, for opening my eyes to your concealed genius and giving me a new look at the World... as well as for all the excitement you bring along with you!"

Second Thoughts

※

In each of us is an element of brilliance.

Sometimes it is perfectly evident and useful, as when someone has an innate, natural understanding of mathematics or demonstrates artistic abilities and prowess.

Sometimes this brilliance, this genius, is not visible; it lies undetected by societal norms or academic systems in the classroom. It lives beneath the surface where it can only be discovered and valued by chance or by deliberate delving and exploring. When someone we might consider not-so-smart displays this kind of brilliance, we often call that person a "late bloomer" or "savant."

The lesson, the challenge, is not only for each of us to recognize a co-worker's or friend's concealed genius but to discover and appreciate that special part of ourselves, as well, and to learn how to apply it successfully.

Dropping In Deeper

1. Why does the author say George is not the "average" guy?

2. What makes everyone turn red while sitting in George's car?

3. Sketch the boys in Malibu approaching the stopped car on the Coast Highway as your mind's eye sees it OR getting a ticket on Malibu Canyon Road. Describe your picture with a caption.

4. What is one way George is able to show his intelligence?

5. Do you have a special skill that changed the way you view the World, just as George's view of ocean waves has changed? Explain.

6. We all have special abilities of one kind or another. Describe an area of "brilliance" in you. Give an example.

7. Describe a time you felt like you were George, a time you weren't aware of something that everyone else seemed to understand.

Chapter 9: Frenemies Forever - *Avoiding Nicotine Addiction In Our Lives*

"**C**an you imagine a culture where people take ground-up leaves, put them in their mouths, set them on fire, and suck on them?" I've asked my students this over the years. They cannot imagine anyone doing this. When I tell them it's our own culture - smokers do it every day -- they're startled. They never think of smoking this way.

Let me pose another related question. Have you ever made a friend of someone your parents didn't care for, someone they didn't want you to spend time with? Then later, did you figure out why they felt that way and perhaps understood their concerns? Maybe this friend eventually became more of an enemy than a friend, a "frenemy." Sometimes we just make bad judgments, poor choices, and then we must figure out how to make things right…if we can.

In the 1950s and 1960s, over half of males in the U.S. were smokers. From the 1950s to the 1960s the number of female smokers rose from around one-quarter to one-third of all women in the U.S.

You may wonder how so many people could ever think that smoking for a lifetime is a great idea. But at that time there is an allure to smoking as ads promoting smoking are everywhere, from TV to billboards to magazines. All the celebrities and talk show hosts are smoking on TV shows and in the movies. In many scenes, when two people enter a living room, the first words spoken by the host are often, "Good to see you! Want a cigarette?"

Everybody's smoking! Go to a restaurant and cigarette smoke drifts over your table and food. At the grocery store moms are smoking as they choose which head of lettuce looks the best. Go for a car ride with Mom and Dad and not only are they smoking but, if it's a cold day, all the windows of the car are rolled up! Ashtrays, often filled with crushed cigarette butts along with their ashes, are in just about everyone's home. Most everyone's clothes, even kids', smell like burnt tobacco all the time. It's the Smoking World.

At this time in the 1960s, smoking is allowed everywhere. This includes even crowd-filled stadiums. At night you can see clouds of smoke floating above the playing field! If you take a ride on a plane it's filled with smoke. The person sitting next to you has a cigarette in hand. A doctor smokes while sitting behind his/her desk giving the patient a diagnosis. Commercials tell people that nine out of ten doctors surveyed prefer Camel cigarettes. TV and radio shows and even family shows in the evening all have cigarette commercials with wonderfully catchy jingles playing during the breaks. It is the Wild West as far as any kind of law and order and truthfulness about the dangers and addiction of smoking is concerned.

As a result, over the years many smokers look upon cigarettes as their "Best Friend." They find they can always depend upon smoking to lessen their anxieties and feel relaxed. It tastes good and for many, it keeps them from gaining weight. That's a good friend!

With smoking in mind, I want to put you in my shoes as an eight-year-old in the middle 1950s so you can understand the minefield we all had to find our way through back then. It wasn't easy.

Mom wants me to do something for her. She gives me 30 cents and says, "Go to the drugstore and get me a pack of cigarettes." Off I go on my ¼ mile walk to the Jack Back's Drug Store, not thinking much of it. I even have a nickel left over for a Three Musketeers candy bar! At the drugstore, there's no issue at all about my age so I give the clerk the 30 cents. I take the pack of cigarettes, and my candy, and head back home. Then I continue on with my little guy day.

I go to the Saturday afternoon matinee at the movie theater. Much of the audience smokes while we watch the characters in the movie smoking. It's just the way things are. I go to the restroom and a nine-year-old kid is smoking. He even asks me if I want a cigarette!

Now I'm a couple of years older. I ride my bike to the bowling alley to meet a friend. Thick cigarette smoke hovers about 6 feet above the lanes. It's no wonder. There's the cigarette vending machine standing right next to the pool tables. A pack of cigarettes comes down the chute for anyone, including children, who has a quarter and can pull a lever. Ashtrays are everywhere, including built-in on every lane.

At home, beside the customary ashtray on the coffee table, there is also a lovely small box. Open it up and there are cigarettes, all neatly laid side-by-side and ready to enjoy. They're always in there. Heck, sometimes it's a music box that plays a cheerful little tune when you lift the lid!

Candy cigarettes and pink bubble gum cigars (traditional ring wrapper included) are anywhere you can buy candy. The "cigarettes" are special because the thin white "cigarette" paper which surrounds the candy contains some powdered sugar which creates "smoke" when a child blows on the candy cigarette as it hangs from her mouth. It would seem children are being groomed to become future smokers.

When kids do craft projects at school or summer camp, one of the most popular is the making of an ashtray for Mom and Dad. A camp counselor never asks, "Do your parents smoke?" If the ashtray is made of clay, we learn how to place our little fingers just right so that we make the proper sized indentations for cigarettes to rest upon. If we're pounding one out of a flat sheet metal disc, we have a specially made mold to use. And of course, if we are at a camp situated near the shore, we learn how to make a seashell into an ashtray. For children back then, the making of ashtrays has become an art form! We're being guided into accepting the World of Smoking as our own World.

That so much of the population of the World smokes is by design. Later, in 1969, with the U.S. Surgeon General's Report, we understand much more about the terrible effects of smoking on the public's health, though the inevitable physical addiction to nicotine is still downplayed by calling smoking a "habit." We also discover that tobacco companies have been paying TV and movie producers to include smoking in their shows and movies – to write in scenes with cigarettes, with the star smoking, whether she does in real life or not.

Eighteen-year-old girls stand on city corners handing out free mini-packs of 3 cigarettes. No one even watches to see if they are given to children. The Zippo lighter makes a special clicking sound every time the cover slides back into place after lighting a cigarette. That sound becomes part of the routine, the experience, of smoking. It's addictive as well.

For many, it's not a matter of "if" you will start smoking, only a matter of "when." Being a smoker is a status symbol for many kids. A popular idea, promoted by showing young movie stars smoking, is that a teenager appears older, more sophisticated, maybe even defiant, with a cigarette in his mouth. Sexy, too. If you see a group of teenagers gathered in a park or a hamburger shop, many of them are smoking. If you're in that group and you don't choose to smoke, lots of times you're looked upon as just being uncool, afraid. It's just that way.

I can't say exactly what keeps a kid from joining in and starting to smoke, especially when everyone else seems to be. We will come to understand, from a psychological perspective, that the ability to wait, to postpone getting or having something, can influence a kid's future. Studies show that those who have a hard time resisting that immediate treat or reward tend to be the ones more likely to give in to the temptation of tobacco. For example, some teenagers can manage to set aside part of their allowance or earned money for something that requires months of saving. It might be a video game, an outfit, or an electric bicycle. These are the people who are less likely to be impulsive and who will not accept that first cigarette when somebody offers it. They won't secretly meet with a classmate to experiment with smoking.

Understand that nicotine is one of the most addictive drugs known to mankind. I will say that again. Nicotine, the principal ingredient in tobacco, is ONE OF THE MOST ADDICTIVE DRUGS KNOWN TO MANKIND! According to Smokefree.gov, nicotine can be as addictive as heroin. It depends upon the individual.

You know that feeling when you bowl a strike or take that first bite into a thick, juicy hamburger or you've just managed to get a date with someone you've always wanted to know? Nicotine has a way of pressing the buttons, the exact receptors in your brain that make you feel good like that. You can get that feeling, over and over again, whenever you send nicotine through your bloodstream to your brain.

Nicotine physically changes receptors in a user's brain, the ones which provide the feeling of pleasure. Those receptors want it again and again, and the user feels uncomfortable until nicotine arrives. This is one aspect of "addiction." This change in the brain's receptors starts after the very FIRST cigarette or anything delivering nicotine. I should note that some people are more susceptible to this change than others. There's no way to tell who will become addicted more easily. And, even if a person quits smoking completely, it takes a long time for those receptors to return to normal. Because the nicotine becomes part of a regular experience — such as after enjoying a meal or just relaxing watching TV — even with the return to normal the former smoker misses the nicotine. Do you really want this in your life?

For over a century, tobacco corporations have worked to hide the health issues related to smoking. Everybody knows that. But that has been a distraction. What they didn't want us to realize is exactly how addictive nicotine can be. Nicotine is addictive to almost everyone, even animals! In laboratories, dogs have been forced to inhale cigarette smoke, and they too have become addicted. It's not a matter of IF you will get addicted to the nicotine in tobacco. It's only a question of how strong your addiction will be. There's no way to know that until you try it. And when you do, in a short time nicotine can become a necessary and expensive part of your life.

My mom was a smoker. She loved cigarettes. She was so addicted that during those many times she TRIED to quit, she told me it was like LOSING HER BEST FRIEND. She didn't die of cancer. She died of a heart attack resulting from emphysema – her lungs, gradually day-by-day, year-by-year getting worse, could no longer take oxygen from the air so she could breathe. In her 60s she was ALWAYS CONNECTED by a tube to an oxygen tank. She slowly strangled. It was like breathing through a scarf, then gradually adding another, and another, until even with an oxygen mask over her face her heart just couldn't take the strain and it failed. This is the way most emphysema victims die.

For some reason not fully understood, smoking makes your blood platelets sticky. Platelets are the red matter in your blood that carry oxygen throughout your body. They clump together in a smoker's veins and arteries, inhibiting blood flow and raising blood pressure. These clumps may break off and float through the bloodstream until they completely clog a heart valve, causing a heart attack, or a blood vessel in the brain, causing a stroke. My dad, a doctor, smoked, too! While standing in line at the bank he had a stroke – a blood vessel in his brain burst. Smoking created blockages in his blood vessels and helped raise his blood pressure to that breaking point. He survived, half-conscious, unable to talk, in a rest home for over a year until he died.

Nobody dies after smoking their first cigarette. But many, after trying that first cigarette, will want another. Eventually, they find themselves addicted. Lots of people live for many years, happily smoking away, and they just adapt to the gradual shortened breath, the rising expense, the smell of tobacco smoke on their breath and clothes, and the continual yearning for a cigarette. Some get cancer of some type or heart disease at a younger age. Some manage to live long lives in spite of smoking. Some develop emphysema. You just cannot predict exactly what effect smoking will have upon you. Do you really need to take the risk of exploring how easily your body becomes addicted to nicotine? Do you really want to take your chances and embark upon a lifelong addiction that, besides being so costly, may cost you your life – or your quality of life?

When I went to high school, going to the restroom often meant smelling cigarette smoke. Besides being annoyed at the smell, I always thought how stupid it was for some kid to risk getting caught smoking just to show off and look macho. I didn't understand that the poor guy was so addicted he HAD to have a cigarette because he was so uncomfortable without one.

Today the school restroom is less likely to smell like cigarette smoke. A lot of kids have figured out that smoking is not a good idea. Their friends are not impressed by someone smoking. If the only way you can impress others is by setting a stick of tobacco on fire and sucking on it...you need to work out another way! Besides that, it is much more expensive than it used to be.

Good news, right? The tobacco corporations have been forced in court to admit that smoking is disastrous to a smoker's health. But the bad news is that they're after YOU in a different way now. There's a minefield out there again for the kids of today because, though things have changed in some ways, in other ways they haven't. Today, a school restroom is more likely to have an unnaturally sweet smell in the air – the sweet smell of the residue of someone exhaling nicotine-laced vapor. So here we go again. A kid gets so addicted to the nicotine from vaping he will risk getting into trouble to feel comfortable for a while. Must we keep doing this?

Vaping looks neat. There's no real smoke. You can carry your vaping device in your pocket like a thumb drive. Vaping "juices" come in many flavors that smell delicious! And there's that allure of the thick vapor smoke exhaled into the air. Vaping can be so inviting, especially since some in the news tell us it's a safer alternative to smoking cigarettes. But it still comes from tobacco. Vaping "juice" still has nicotine. There is MUCH MORE NICOTINE in the vaping "juice" than in a cigarette, which means the user becomes more deeply addicted.

Vaping hasn't been around long enough for us to fully understand its long-term effects on the body. Vaping does not have all the toxins created from burning tobacco, but there are other kinds of toxins, and vaping still provides the nicotine from tobacco, just like cigarettes. Studies are starting to show problems with lung function and complete lung failure when different compounds are vaped – such as ones that contain Vitamin E or have THC, the principal ingredient in marijuana.

Maybe you can sympathize with how so many people allow themselves to become addicted to nicotine through smoking, vaping, chewing tobacco, or using snuff. It can be so easy to fall into that trap and not be able to escape.

Mom and Dad, learning to smoke their first cigarette as young people, had no idea they were headed for addiction. In those days, there was no warning and little awareness that because of smoking, their futures could include emphysema, heart disease, brain damage, and the potential for cancers all over the body.

But we do realize this now. We don't have to keep making the same mistake of getting ourselves addicted to nicotine. We can understand how not to give in to that first impulse, that temptation to experiment with anything containing nicotine.

The tobacco and vaping corporations that are creating vaping devices are hiding things again! Vaping, like smoking, is HIGHLY ADDICTIVE. That means that once you start, even if you manage to quit, for the rest of your life you may ALWAYS feel, like my mom, that YOU HAVE LOST YOUR BEST FRIEND– you will wish you could vape or have a cigarette just one more time.

Her "Best Friend" was actually her frenemy.

As a kid, I knew disappointment. I may not have received the birthday gift I had hoped for or the position on the football team I had tried so hard to earn.

But that's okay. That kind of disappointment I may not totally forget, but I can look back upon it now and smile because I've moved on.

But vapers, smokers, chew, and snuff users know the disappointment of trying to quit, trying to give it up, only to relapse, to fall back and give in to the addiction to nicotine once again. Look at all the "Here's How to Quit Smoking" ads you see on TV. Escape is so difficult. It rules their lives.

Nicotine can become the vapers' and smokers' secret "Best Friend"...the kind of poorly chosen friend your parents tried to warn you about. If you accept nicotine into your life, you will have made a frenemy... forever.

Second Thoughts

※

Don't try vaping. Don't try smoking. Don't try snuff or chew...even once. You will most likely pay the price if you do - for your lifetime.

Dropping In Deeper

1. We understand no one dies from trying just one cigarette. But name two risks of trying smoking or vaping just one time.

2. Why is the author, as a little boy, allowed to buy cigarettes at the drugstore?

3. If you were a kid back in the 1950s, would you likely have experimented with smoking? Why or why not?

4. Why does the author call the time he was growing up "a minefield?"

5. Why would tobacco companies give away free cigarettes?

6. What effect does smoking have upon blood platelets?

7. Have you ever felt like you were uncool or afraid when you chose not to do something others were doing? Describe the situation and how you handled it.

8. Does smoking/vaping have a different appeal to girls than boys? Explain.

9. What does the word "relapse" mean as in "...trying to give it

up only to relapse..."? Describe some time in your life when you or someone you know relapsed in some way.

10. What is an important lesson YOU learned from reading this story? What makes it important to you?

11. What traits might make a person more likely to become a nicotine user?

12. Why is the author so against nicotine use? Provide an example from your life that demonstrates the author's point.

Chapter 10: Sidehill Badger - *Coping With Worry & Fear*

Many of the events occurring back during my college years are as if they're in a fog that requires I flip on my car's windshield wipers – it's so difficult to recall them, to see them clearly now. But just as you don't forget driving through an intersection in thick fog and just catching a glimpse of the red light overhead you never saw in time, so I remember a particular event as a counselor for a YMCA camp in the Sierra Nevada Mountains. It is pretty special, and unforgettable.

As a first-year counselor, I've been given an assignment. It's for me to surprise the whole camp of nine- to twelve-year-old boys early in the morning. So, just before reveille, I'm running along the slope of the hill just behind the sleeping campers' cabins screaming "Badger! Sidehill badger! Ow!" I disappear into the administration cabin.

At breakfast time I stagger into the dining hall. My left forearm overflows with gauze as some fresh red oozes out. The kids' loud voices downshift to a hush as I seat myself beside some of the campers.

Then comes the rumble of comments -- "What happened to him? How bad is it? Is he going to be okay?" -- the whole place forgets about breakfast – for about 20 seconds.

During announcements after the meal, I share the bad news and the good news. The bad news is, of course, that a sidehill badger has attacked me. The good news is that it has been captured.

"Sidehill badger? Is that like a beaver? More like a small bear? Anything resembling a mountain lion?" the campers wonder.

Sensing the growing concern and confusion, I address the assembled 9 to 12 year old boys. "I spotted this sidehill badger approaching one of the cabins and gave chase to it. But it turned on me and bit my arm. Fortunately, as it was about to attack me again, and since its right-side legs are shorter than its left-side legs, perfect for running to the left on a hill, it changed direction, lost its balance, fell over and tumbled. That's when several of the other counselors were able to catch it. We have it trapped in a container up at the baseball diamond. The whole camp is going up there after breakfast to take care of it."

Indeed, the all dirt field seems an ideal location for a confrontation such as this.

Shortly after this we all hustle to the all-dirt baseball diamond. About 100 young campers, along with their counselors, are shoulder-to-shoulder, three people deep, in a circle around the pitcher's mound.

Perched on the mound is an old gray, galvanized metal washtub, turned upside-down. Underneath it waits "The Creature." No one knows what it looks like except for a couple of counselors and me.

"Everybody pick up something to protect yourself!" shouts one of the counselors from a megaphone. Everyone does – rocks and sticks are all in hand.

They're all wondering if this will be their last moment on Earth. After all, it has attacked one of the counselors and all the adults are in fear of it. Thoughts run through the crowd, "I love my mom. I miss my little brother!" But no one chooses to leave the circle. There is strength in numbers.

Instructions follow as to what to do if the vicious sidehill badger should come their way. The basic message is, "Fight for your life!"

Another counselor, armed with a long tree branch, stealthily approaches the tub at the center of attention. We are all holding our breath. Nobody dares blink. Everybody has his "owl eyes" on high. There's not a sound coming from inside the washtub. We know IT is just waiting for its chance to get at us.

The counselor slips the end of the branch under the lip of the tub, then stops and turns his head, surveying the group to be certain everyone is prepared for the impending danger. Total silence is the order of the day.

He flips the tub over and dashes away to save his own life. The washtub does a somersault as it flies off the mound, clattering as it lands a few feet away. Nothing moves. There's a groan from the crowd.

Now we can see a plain old gray metal bucket, the kind you may have filled with water at one time and swung around, up and over your head, managing somehow to keep the water inside of it. The bucket lies upside-down, its handle buried in the dirt off to one side.

The tension drops a notch. But big trouble still lurks under the bucket. Okay, so the creature may be a bit smaller than the tyrannosaurus rex roaring in our imaginations. As our eyes can be bigger than our stomachs, so can our fears make circumstances larger than life.

The Attack of the Sidehill Badger: Take 2.

Again, the counselor creeps up toward the hillside monster. Again, the circle of boys, rocks and sticks in hand, primordial instincts kicking in, prepares for the kill – whichever way it may go. Again, silence demands its due. And again, no noise, no stirring, not even any rustling emanates from the creature's cramped domain. All is quiet beneath the bucket.

The counselor doesn't dare attempt to just slip the tip of the branch again under the lip of the bucket. Instead, he delicately guides the branch until it curls up under the bucket's handle. This time there is no cause to pause. Everyone knows the procedure.

With fluid motion, as if he has performed this task many times before, the counselor swings the bucket up and again streaks for the safety of the crowd...

So many of us share the fear that somewhere in the great hills, mountains, and valleys of the Sierras or some local mountains there lies a monster just waiting to get us. If we go roaming alone somewhere up there in the moonlight, IT will find US. And if IT doesn't have the time or inclination, a flying saucer filled with extraterrestrials most certainly will be on our trail. We don't have a chance.

But here, in the bright sunlight of mid-morning, what faces us, and all the fears we possess, collectively from all the frightful experiences we have known in all our lives, sits a bag. It's a paper bag, large enough for a sandwich and some potato chips.

Heads tilt sideways as the murmur of the confused boys rises in intensity.

The counselor walks over to the bag. He picks it up by its folded-over top. He opens it wide and reaches in without hesitation. He pulls out an empty, lidless glass jar of Hellman's Mayonnaise. But anyone can see that the lip portion, where the cap would normally screw on, is partially shattered, and makes the container useless.

It's the badger. The badger? No, the "bad jar." The sidehill badger now reveals itself to be only a broken mayonnaise jar...a bad jar.

Thirty minutes later, back in their cabins preparing for the day's adventures to follow, many campers are still shaking their heads, truly not understanding what just happened. They had bravely faced fear in its worst form, as the great unknown, and had come out unscathed and unhurt. But many are still confused, still wondering what did happen to that counselor (me) with his hand all bloody from the sidehill badger attack? They haven't quite realized, yet, that this was just a skit, a trick, a performance meant to add some excitement to their summer camp experience.

Someday they will understand. And they will most likely pass the skit on to others – in a version encompassing and embracing many of their own versions of fear. These kids, as grown-ups, will find ways to give others the opportunity to conquer, in a fun way, that fear of the unknown. How memorable is that!

Second Thoughts

※

How many times have you worried about something, or been afraid of something, and then it turned out to be not such a big deal? You arrived at the conclusion that your fears were greater than necessary and you made a big deal out of a small matter.

Worry and fear are necessary or else sometimes we can walk into a terrible situation blind and ignorant and ripe for the worst. But we must contain that worry and fear. There must be limits. One of those limits involves not letting our imagination to run the show. Just as the camp staff trapped the sidehill badger in a tub, a bucket, and then a lunch bag, only to soon reveal it to be a broken glass jar, so can we find our way to managing our fears of the unknown. The campers had the freedom to leave, but chose to stay there, facing the monster together.

There needs to be a balance between the worst-case scenario and what else we might expect to happen. Experience with handling fear within a safe environment helps prepare us for the challenges that are coming our way.

Dropping In Deeper

1. What do all the campers think when the counselor comes staggering into the dining hall? Was that really blood on his arm? If not, what do you suppose it was?

2. What's a fear in your own life? How do you handle it?

3. How wise might it be to discuss a worry or fear you have with a family member, friend, or professional (teacher, priest/rabbi, counselor)? How would you begin?

4. What does "stealthily" mean as in "...stealthily approaches the tub...?" Use it in a sentence.

5. Sketch all the campers surrounding the sidehill badger in the tub as your mind's eye sees it OR the camp counselor staggering into breakfast. Describe your picture with a caption.

6. As a young person yourself, who is someone you admire for the way she or he handles problems? What makes that person's approach so special?

7. How can you help a friend who appears worried?

8. The author writes, "We all know that somewhere in the great hills...there lies a monster waiting just to get us." What does he

mean? Is it true? Why or why not?

9. What if this was a girls' camp? Do you think girls would be as likely to stand around in a circle to have to face the sidehill badger? Why or why not?

Chapter 11: Submarines, The Silent Service Days –
Adolescent Anxiety & Depression

I'm seventeen. As I'm about to graduate high school, go to the beach, take my girlfriend on a date, play football, bag groceries at the supermarket, mess around with the guys, and just live life, there is something always, always in the back of my mind, like an app running in the background on a computer.

There is a war going on. Congress doesn't call it that. In Washington it's referred to as a "conflict." But it's an all-out war on the ground, in the air, and on the water in Vietnam. Those of us guys graduating high school and turning eighteen must register with the Selective Service – the draft board – and then dread getting that letter beginning with these fateful words: "GREETING: You are hereby ordered for induction into the

Armed Forces of the United States..."

All of us have buddies or schoolmates who have already gone to Vietnam. Some are dead. Others are disfigured due to mortar attacks, grenades, landmines, guns, bazookas, napalm, and on and on. Some return physically unharmed; but the damage may be deeper, unseen. Their personality is no longer the same. It has turned dark...very dark.

We don't even understand why our country is in this war or why we're going there. There are no enemy North Vietnamese coming by land, sea or air to invade the U.S. We hear it has something to do with protecting Democracy. We hear about the "Domino Theory," something about Communism spreading from China to Vietnam to Indonesia and beyond. Who knows? In previous decades France sent troops to fight in Vietnam but they were forced out. The French left in such a hurry that they abandoned their battlefield equipment!

Most of us don't want to go. But we have no choice. If we get that letter, then for two years we must serve wherever Uncle Sam sends us. For most of us, it's Vietnam.

I don't mean to bum you out, but that's how things are at this time. We're just kids slowly turning into adults – some more slowly than others. We're making plans, in my case, going to college and surfing (or maybe the other way around). I'm not the kind who can focus on several things at one time. Can you relate to that? My best work occurs when I can work on one project or subject, complete it, and then move on to the next. For me, at this point in time, I focus on surfing...then my girlfriend...then college. They're a challenge to manage together.

Setting Vietnam aside, my goal is to have a part-time job to support myself while I go to school, to soon marry my girlfriend, to hang around with my friends, and to figure out this thing called "Life." To be sincere, I really DON'T want to go to college right now; at seventeen my devotion is surfing. But I'll follow the crowd and join the many heading right back into the classroom after finishing high school. I have no idea what career I should pursue. But by going to college, the government allows me a 2-S Deferment, meaning I won't get drafted until I finish – as long as I keep my grades up.

But I don't. No one talks to me about how to schedule my classes and I don't know enough to ask a counselor or someone smarter how and what to do. So, every Monday, Wednesday, and Friday I have English 101 at 8:00 A.M., Music Appreciation at 10:30, and Sociology I at 1:00. On Tuesdays and Thursdays, I have an equally spread-out schedule of different classes.

There isn't enough time to go back home between classes and I don't push myself to go to the library. Since I'm a single-tasker, if I'm going to classes, don't expect me to break my momentum and go to the library. It's just who I am.

Instead, I take a nap in my 1966 VW camper van, the one my dad helped me get so I wouldn't buy a motorcycle. He worries about my safety on the road, so he bribes me with this offer. Fair enough. I'll stay away from motorcycles. I sleep fine at night, so it's not clear why I feel a nap between classes is a good idea. Maybe it's just easier than studying. Maybe it just helps me cope with everything around me and in the news.

The van has my surfboard in it, always ready to head to the beach. As you can guess, I often give in to temptation and skip out on my classes in order to go surfing. Soon my grades are at the bottom of the tank, and I know I could shortly lose my deferment from the draft. I am worried about things...but I still can't get myself to study and attend classes regularly. I don't know why. I just can't!

Another activity besides surfing is sneaking into the Greek Theater to see concerts for free – it's fun and fairly easy. The Greek is a well-known amphitheater in Los Angeles surrounded by hillsides filled with trees and chapparal; the famous Griffith Observatory is right up the road. You've likely seen that observatory in movies and TV shows.

In the dark of night, my girlfriend and I hike into the hills to sneak in through a hole cut in the fence, and trek down into the cover of the trees to watch the concerts. Sometimes, the park rangers turn on giant sprinklers just outside the fence to discourage us, but we make it through and find a spot to nestle in, hidden in the shadows and foliage.

Most times it feels like we're tucked in there alone. Often, we see no one in the trees with us, but then there's a "Crack!" as someone steps on a fallen tree branch somewhere – louder than the din of the concert crowd below us. When the house lights dim, we feel protected enough to climb out from behind the tree, onto an open spot of earth to see better. Major artists such as Neil Diamond, The Temptations, and Johnny Mathis perform at the Greek. One night, at the beginning of Harry Belafonte's concert, he yells, "Hello Orchestra Section!"

Those in the orchestra section respond, "Hello!" He calls out to every other section, waiting for their response.

After the back row, Belafonte cups his hands shouting, "Hello Tree People!"

There is a startling roar of "Hello!" from all around us! We have no idea there are so many other people up there on that dark hillside!

Security guards, wearing white jackets and carrying flashlights, quietly search through the trees and the bushes for intruders. I have been caught once, and quietly escorted down to the back wall of the amphitheater to the front entrance. It's too much of a hassle to go through the whole hike-in again, so I just head home.

I mention the security guards because, while hiding in the trees, I can't help thinking about being drafted and, instead of hiking in the park, hiding somewhere in the Vietnam jungle surrounded by camouflaged Vietcong carrying weapons – searching through the undergrowth to slaughter me. Or maybe I'm about to shoot them. Ugly thoughts like this keep flashing through my head at The Greek. I try to suppress them but can't control such imaginings; they come and go whenever they want.

There's also my part-time job. Working at the grocery store as a bagger may help with money, but reporting for work right after surfing is not the best idea. I wear my uniform, a white, short-sleeved dress shirt and red store vest. Sometimes, when I lean over someone's grocery cart to organize the cans and stuff, without warning ocean water suddenly gushes out of my nose! It's a side-effect of surfing. I know… gross!

It's here, at the market, I meet Joel. He's a checker on the night crew. Joel's older, maybe 22 or so. It's hard to tell because he's already balding. He has lots of ideas and is full of sarcastic humor. Sometimes we rag on each other, seeing who can give the best insults. But you never want to get into a "chop" session with him because he always wins. Joel seems to like me. At times after work, we hang out. He has a beige 1963 VW bug with a strip of embossed red tape across the glove box which reads, "DO NOT OPEN DOORS OR WINDOWS AT SPEEDS IN EXCESS OF 120 MPH." That's his kind of humor.

One day he says to me, "Pete, I know you're worried about getting drafted. How about joining the Navy reserves?"

"What do you mean? There's a long waiting list to get into the reserves and I don't have a chance." Lots of guys are trying to get into the Navy reserves these days because it's only a two-year stint, not the four-year regular Navy enlistment. We figure if you're in the Navy there's not much chance of having to crawl through the Vietnam jungle.

"Yeah, there's a long list for the regular reserves," he agrees, "but not for the submarine service. They call it, 'the Silent Service' because you hear very little about it and you work underwater. You must volunteer. No one can be forced to be a submariner."

"Wow!" I'm thinking, being in a submarine must mean you're a long way from the Vietnam jungle and napalm.

Without any hesitation I jump, imploring him, "Where do I sign up?"

Without discussing the matter with anyone but my girlfriend, within a month or so I take a qualifying test, sign up and attend my induction at the Long Beach Naval Station, and just before turning 19, I leave for a six-week submarine boot camp in San Francisco. When my parents discover I've enlisted they're really upset. "You should have stayed in school!" they bark at me. They don't understand I'm apt to get drafted because of my low grades.

On the first day of boot camp the Navy trainers put 30 of us in a classroom and run a 16 mm film produced by CBS. It's a TV special entitled, "The Legacy of the Thresher," a report about a U.S. nuclear submarine which imploded on the ocean bottom, losing its entire crew. Nobody really knows what caused the sub to crash dive until the ocean water pressure destroyed it. I think the Navy shows us the film to shake us up a little and maybe weed out anyone who is uncertain about committing to the submarine service. It doesn't get to me. But I will never forget the photos of chunks of the submarine's hull resting at the bottom of the depths of the ocean. The pressure down that deep is enormous.

Eight months later, still 19, I commence my two years of active duty. Leaving my girl, now my fiancée, is not great, but it means I have a better chance of surviving this damn war. So be it.

You may be saying, "Whoa! You're like an out-of-control freight train! One moment you're hiking the Griffith Park hills and soon after you're headed to a Navy submarine! Are you thinking any of this through? Are you sure you'll adapt well to living underwater in close quarters like that?" My friends ask me the same questions.

Do I consider all of this? No. I'm an impulsive guy. I just see this as a solution to my immediate fears about surviving the war and I go for it, rather like jumping on the first set of rocks I see to cross a stream. Maybe I make it. Maybe I get my shoes wet. I could decide to survey around the bend and check things out a bit, but that's not my way. I go for it like when I go for a wave -- sometimes even though it's huge and might not be "makeable," I drop in. But life feels so chaotic these days.

At home during dinner we see the war unfold every night on the news. We hear the "kill count" of enemy troops – numbers someone has undoubtedly just made up. There are also reports about the anti-war movement with its marches and protests. The country is so divided. A guy is a "draft dodger" if he finds some way out of getting drafted, but when a soldier returns from Vietnam, he's spat upon and hated for being a killer of innocent people! You can't win.

At the same time, there is a lot of racial unrest dividing the country even further. People march and sometimes riot against racial inequality in America, while others taunt and attack them.

And there's ample news of illegal drug use. You can get years in jail for being caught with marijuana. It's crazy times, and I'm sucked up into this tornado of hate and confusion. Maybe there are some good reasons why we're in this war. I just don't know but I want to believe our leaders are telling us the truth. I don't feel like I have much control over my life. Joining the Navy frees me from some of this chaos and pressure, so I can just focus on serving out my two years. I take that step onto the next rock across the stream.

For 18–19-year-olds, particularly males, this is a difficult period for another reason. It's rarely discussed, but at this age a person who has behaved normally can suddenly develop serious mental illness issues. For instance, bipolar behavior with radical mood swings - boundless energy followed by days of sleeping and depression - can appear in the late teen years. The same can be said of schizophrenia with an onset of delusions, hallucinations, and difficult behavior. It's unclear why this occurs. These conditions do not afflict me, of course, but still, there is so much turmoil in my life – and in the lives of all late adolescents in the 1960s. It's chaotic. It's depressing.

I report to the Long Beach Naval Station to commence active duty and await orders to a submarine. I see some Marines in battle fatigues marching by and ask a guy next to me, "What are Marines are doing here?"

He answers, "Those aren't Marines. They're Navy heading to 'Nam."

"What? I thought being in the Navy meant being onboard ships and stuff like that!"

He concludes, "Yeah, but it also means you can get stationed at the naval support base at Da Nang in Vietnam. Some guys get river patrol boat (PBR) duty in the Mekong Delta where they ride in fast-moving fiberglass hull boats looking for Viet Cong. It just depends on where Uncle Sam decides to put you."

Suddenly, my vision (and idealized version) of the Navy changes right on the spot. No longer do I feel "snug as a bug in a rug," protected from having to go to Vietnam. I'm so glad I'm getting a submarine! I don't know how I'd handle getting sent over there.

My orders come in. I'm assigned to the USS Baya, AGSS-318, a 1940s diesel submarine, not a modern nuclear one. But I get the last laugh. It's based in San Diego, not far from my home in Los Angeles. Better than that, it's a research vessel loaded with all kinds of sonar research equipment and computers. In a couple of months, we will head for the South Pacific Ocean, around Pago Pago and Tahiti, for our scientific work. To take on supplies, our boat must dock at numerous locations, first stop Hawaii. It's about a six-month deployment. Talk about lucky! Here a war is going on and I'm headed to tropical paradise! What a way to serve my country!

Yes, but to paraphrase an old saying, "Every silvery, sunshiny day has a bank of clouds waiting just below the horizon."

Let's talk a bit about submarine life. When you see a submariner wearing silver or gold dolphins on her/his chest, that represents a tremendous level of responsibility and commitment. It means that person has studied and worked to achieve their rank as a seaman, second class petty officer or officer. But far beyond this, that person has studied and memorized their assigned submarine. In total darkness, he/she can locate and operate essential valves, switches, and equipment in the nine compartments of the boat!

Why? Right to the end of WWII, a battle scene involving a submarine did not always include the captain looking through a periscope and ordering, "Fire number one torpedo!" Because it needed to recharge batteries using its diesel engines or else go dead in the water, a submarine sometimes had to surface and fire its 25-caliber deck guns. It was necessary for each crew member to know everything about the boat and understand other crew members' jobs so that losing someone didn't mean losing control of the boat. By passing tests based upon this knowledge requirement, a submariner receives the dolphin pin. It really is a proud moment!

Back to me…remember, the fellow who can't or won't even study between classes in college? Now I'm onboard a submarine, and it's a whole new world. I understand that I must work on earning rank; as an enlistee, I must study to advance from being a "seaman" to a "petty officer."

At the same exact time I'm expected to become "submarine qualified," to work on learning my boat and passing tests to earn my silver dolphin. This can take several months to achieve, depending upon how studious and intelligent a person is. I'm not permitted much free time until I qualify. The USS Baya will not depart for a couple of months, so I have time, and the guys onboard will assist me. There's a code of honor and support shared by submariners. Still, I can feel the pressure.

We do have normal workdays during the week. As a lowly recruit, my responsibilities vary – I polish the brass on the hatches of the torpedo tubes, chip off old paint on the hull and repaint, and clean compartments including the head (toilet). Study time occurs before or after the workday, and on weekends.

For well over a month, I portion my time, part of it studying to advance to petty officer, and part focusing on the study guide for the boat. It's getting really difficult. I can't find a balance and don't seem to be making much progress.

I'm nineteen. I worry that I won't make it. My fiancée is back at home in Los Angeles, and I want to see her. Whenever I figure I have time over the weekend, I make the hour-and a-half journey up there, even if it's only to spend a couple of hours with her. But this means lost study time. This may sound to you a bit like my jetting off to the beach instead of studying between college classes. Since I can't keep a car on base, I must take the bus or train up, and usually, because of the late hour I return, I hitchhike back. That means arriving back to base about 1:00 A.M. I'm a mess the next day. I'm losing it. But there is hope. We're headed out to sea for a few days of sea trials, and I figure I can catch up on both my submarine qualifications and studies then.

Finally, everything comes together, but not in a good way.

In preparation for departing, our boat churns out for several days of sea trials in the waters down south off of Baja, Mexico. This is to make certain the boat and crew are ready for the voyage ahead. Just before we commence our first dive, in the berthing compartment a crew member ties a piece of string onto a valve handle on one side of the bulkhead (wall) and connects it to one on the other side. He makes it taut, like a miniature tightrope in a circus. As the submarine submerges a couple hundred feet, the string sags, almost touching the deck! I can't believe how the water pressure compresses the hull so that our boat shrinks as the bulkheads move inward. Upon surfacing, the string becomes taut once again. I'm a little shaken by this.

Unfortunately, for the last three days of our five-day sea trial, we've had to endure a tropical storm with heavy swells and terrible conditions. Just as unfortunate, because the USS Baya is an auxiliary submarine which can't submerge and run on just its batteries for more than 24 hours, we must ride out the storm on the surface. This is unlike a nuclear sub which would submerge in the calm of the depths the entire time.

We can't dive because there is tremendous danger if we should have to surface during a storm – a swell could hit the side of the boat as it is rising at an angle and cause it to capsize. The 254 lead-acid battery cells installed on the boat's bottom could break loose, pouring out acid and creating chlorine gas. This could kill the crew in an explosion.

Riding out a three-day storm on the ocean's surface in a 330-foot-long submarine is wretched. It rolls and shakes and wobbles non-stop. No one onboard can hold down their food, even the captain. We're all sitting with our butts on the deck and our backs against the bulkhead, hovering over anything we can barf into. It's bread and water for those trying days.

We must, of course, man our duty stations during our work time. I'm assigned as the helmsman, meaning I turn the wheel that steers the rudder. It's quite a task in heavy seas, but I manage. We all have our responsibilities. But now, I can't study on my off-hours due to the awful conditions. My plan to "catch up" on my "quals" turns into nothing but misery!

We return to Ballast Point, the submarine base on Point Loma in San Diego. Everyone is in bad shape, even the boat! The paint we used on the hull to cover the orange primer has failed. The sub looks like something from the classic TV show McHale's Navy, with comical jagged orange patches where the paint let go. They stand out against the rest of the dark gray paint making the boat look like it should be renamed the "USS Tigger" from Winnie the Pooh. It's quite a sight and I'm in worse shape than the boat, trying to recover and bummed about falling behind even more on my studies.

It's now late at night the first day back and I'm in my submarine bunk in the darkened berth. I've pushed aside the plastic bunk cover which keeps diesel engine fumes from settling into the fabric of the bed. When I sleep on my back, there's about a 12" clearance between my nose and the bottom of the steel bunk above me. As I try to rest, my mind flashes over my current predicament.

Submarine qualifying...leaving my girl...may head to Vietnam if I don't make it...still recovering from the rough weather sea trials ...working on petty officer requirements...President Nixon talking about ending the war...not surfing...students protesting the war...parents giving me a hard time about joining the Navy...loneliness...away from home and friends...wondering what my career will be...not talking to anyone about my worries and the frustration...so unhappy. I can't see any sunlight ahead, only clouds. And there's certainly no "silver lining" to them.

Suddenly, in the darkness, I'm crying, uncontrollably, like a little child. Just as the USS Thresher dived too deep with the underwater pressure crushing it, the pressures surrounding me cause me to collapse and dive into a darkness, a depression I've never known. I don't see how I can do all of this. I had it made. Now, I'm going to lose everything. I don't see that next rock to step on to make it across the stream.

I'm out of control. A couple of the crew members try to help and eventually calm me down as best they can. Soon I'm back in my bunk, but I've changed. I'm looking for a way out. I've decided to leave the submarine service. With that quick decision, I've found that next rock to step on to make it.

The submarine service is voluntary. A submarine sailor can get reassigned to "surface" duty. However, to bail out on your submarine and its crew, to "Non-Vol," is serious, and the crew resents you. That camaraderie, that feeling of shared purpose and unity, turns into hate for a guy who jumps ship. I understand this, but I can't worry about it now.

The captain sends me to the base psychiatrist who is also a submariner. He's a great guy and listens to my story empathetically. I am assigned a bunk at the base barracks as I go through the process of reassignment, and I work in an office as a typist. It's great except I know the crew of the boat now despises me. But the doctor and I get along so well that soon I'm having dinner with him and his family. He surfs, too, so on our off time we end up surfing Point Loma together! Things look promising. I've found a way out, again.

Ah, but there's a storm brewing not far ahead. Yes, I DO find the base psychiatrist, who makes himself available to talk to me about everything. But DO I LISTEN to him? Do I value what he says and weigh what I'm set on doing, leaving the submarine service vs. what he offers, working through my issues and finding a way to remain onboard? No, out of panic and urgency to get away from it all, I don't listen. I just want to run and be free of all of this as quickly as possible. I ignore any opportunity to resolve matters. I sign the papers permitting me to leave the submarine service. With that signature, I give permission for a lot of chaos and pain to come my way.

There are still times I must report to the boat for duty reasons. One of the crew says to me, "The last guy who Non-Volled got PBR duty in Vietnam." Now I'm scared out of my mind as I wait week after week for my orders. My anxiety rises again and takes hold; I'm just a zombie, doing what I must on base, and not of much use to anyone, including my girl.

In about a month my orders come through. I'm assigned to the Communications Unit at Naval Station Midway Island, a tiny island (actually, two atolls) in the middle of the Pacific Ocean serving as a communications link to Asia and a sea and air rescue station. It's also a bird sanctuary with imported dirt and trees throughout. Midway was made famous by the battle there during WWII. It's the land of deserted white coral beaches surrounded by aqua blue water and gooney birds. Happily, it lies over a thousand miles from Vietnam. I'm truly a lucky guy!

A few weeks later I fly to Hawaii and then catch a chartered military flight to the island. I report to the master chief in the communications building who tells me that my evaluation from my former submarine stinks, but he will give me a second chance. I work hard to show him the person I truly am. It goes great!

The Navy offers correspondence courses which provide studies I can apply toward a college degree. I'm inspired. My master chief in the communications unit is a gruff guy, but he's fair. He's famous for being tough on everyone. I'm basically a custodian, waxing the deck areas and running the buffer, painting, clearing up his desk, etc. This includes removing and washing out his coffee cup which overflows with tobacco spit. He appreciates my good attitude, my willingness to work, and talks to me abou following in his footsteps by studying to be an electronics technician.

I explain to him that I'm interested in going back to school when I finish my enlistment, and he respects that. In fact, when President Nixon comes to Midway Island for talks with South Vietnamese President Thieu regarding plans to end the Vietnam War, the chief honors me by assigning me as a driver in the welcoming parade. I'm one of only two personnel from our entire unit given such an honor! President Thieu gives each of us involved a special, silver with gold emblem lighter to commemorate the event. I've never had use for the thing, but I still have it.

My inspiration to study is due in part to the chief's belief in me. But it also comes from the lousy characters I've known and worked under in the Navy. While the chief is an exception, many others boss everyone around, some even carrying a coffee cup on their belt. They like to be told exactly when to get up and what to do. Their home is the Navy. I don't know if they could manage to cope in the everyday world of being a civilian. They're quick to tell you what to do, and if you have a suggestion or concern, they're not interested.

An example would be the paint job on the USS Baya. Those of us applying the primer knew something was wrong because it would not dry completely – it remained sticky, like there was honey on top of it. But the boatswain's mate (our boss) ignored our observations. So, we painted over the primer with the dark gray hull paint. That's how we ended up with the "USS Tigger", orange strips and all. My inspiration becomes to never be like those guys – people who have difficulty running their own life but want to tell me how to live mine.

I work on the courses in my free time. I'm assigned to Midway Island for a year, and when that is through, I will have only seven months left in the service. I could elect to remain there to the end of my enlistment, and President Nixon is giving Navy reservists like me "early-outs," meaning he's cutting short the enlistment time for those in the reserves to lower military spending. If I wait, I could qualify for that and might get back to my fiancée early. I only need to be patient.

But I have what I figure to be a better plan. Since going to Vietnam is a twelve-month commitment, I'm safe from that, so I'll leave paradise and put in for new orders. I could end up in San Diego or Long Beach!

New orders come in all right...back to the USS Baya, my old submarine!

Let's consider my situation. I could return to the USS Baya, and since I Non-Volled, probably get put in the barracks as before. I could spend my last months in the Navy working in an office in San Diego and getting up to see my girl on weekends, maybe surfing Point Loma again with the base psychiatrist.

But I don't stop to consider all of this.

Without talking to anyone (sound familiar?), without thinking about anything except the fear and trauma I remember from my submarine days and how those guys hate me, I immediately jump at the first rock I spot, that idea about a way out of this, and I tell the yeoman (clerk), "That's not right! I'm not submarine-qualified anymore. I can't be assigned a submarine. The Navy has made a mistake."

You don't tell the Navy it made a mistake. What I don't realize is that the Navy looks upon that as a refusal of orders...not a good idea. I end up, instead, on a ship immediately deploying to the Gulf of Tonkin in Vietnam.

A ship's overseas deployment can be around nine months. The Navy figures that it will fly me back home when my enlistment is over. But I have issues here again, too. While driving a lieutenant back to our ship from the airport at night during a heavy Seattle rainstorm, he must grab the wheel to keep me from steering us into a head-on crash on a freeway onramp. I'm accustomed to one-way ramps. At this time in Seattle, ramps are two-way with no center divider, just a yellow line...hard to see on a soaking wet night. As a result, I am bumped off the elite driver unit. I work on the deck crew tending oil lines on the ship and then get reassigned to assist the chaplain in the ship's library. It's a wonderful job. When I qualify for a three month "early out" to attend college, I have a California senator attempt to assist me in getting off the ship. However, the ship's executive officer doesn't believe in "early outs" for college, so I must remain.

What else? My fiancée stops writing to me and I have no idea why. I escape from a crazy bar gal in the Philippines who tries to stab me to death. One day while off the coast of Vietnam, I have the flu and get transported by copter to a nearby aircraft carrier for medical attention. I assume the sickbay personnel will inform the chaplain, so I tell no one. Hours later I can't be found since I'm still on the carrier waiting to visit the doctor. A ship-wide search for me takes place because I'm thought to be lost at sea! Instead of library duty, I get reassigned and finish off the last three months of my enlistment cleaning up in the crew's mess hall. I spend entire paychecks on overseas phone calls to my girl only to hear sobbing at the other end of the line. I find upon my return home that my "fiancée" is into an office romance. She decides not to send me a "Dear John" letter because I might do "something desperate!" Oh man, I lose the girl, almost my mind, but…I survive.

So, let's review my two years spent in the Navy in my quest to avoid service in Vietnam:

- I get orders to a submarine heading to exotic ports in the South Pacific, but instead choose to "Non-Vol" from the USS Baya.

- At my next duty station, Midway Island, I must overcome a horrible evaluation from my former submarine.

- So that I might qualify for an "early out," I intentionally remain as valueless to the Navy as possible by staying the same rank and then tell the Navy it made a mistake when new orders reassign me to the USS Baya in San Diego.

- I receive new orders to the USS Sacramento, immediately deploying to Vietnam.

During my two years in the Navy, I COULD HAVE: realized that I work better doing things one-at-a time and only concentrated on qualifying for my submarine, THEN worked on becoming a petty officer. I don't recall anyone suggesting this to me -- although someone may have, and I just failed to listen.

In summary, I miss out on a dream trip to the South Pacific and returning in six months to San Diego. My fiancée ends up marrying a guy in her office. I end up in Vietnam (off the coast), anyway!

Some of my choices are abrupt and impulsive because I'm suffering from "free floating" anxiety. I just don't know how to cope with the matters of the day. Those clouds without silver linings surround me and I can't find a way out.

I must find a way to work through the clouds, not out of them, by dealing with the issues rather than just trying to escape. Essentially, I don't know how to share my troubles with anyone and get good advice or discover a solution with which I can live. There are other groups of rocks, other paths, to choose to make it across the stream. I must be patient and look for them, not just jump at the first ones I see.

I do choose a way of expressing my feelings...in poems and songs. I write about losing my girl and how it feels. It helps me reconnect with myself and I find how to cope.

Through all of this I do accomplish something. Towards the end of my enlistment, I work through those clouds, the depression, feeling overwhelmed by the pressures of the times and the fallout from some of my stupid, hasty decisions. Upon the completion of my enlistment, I enter college with numerous credits which count towards graduation; this time around I hit the books and make the Dean's List.

I can't help but wonder…what if? What if I were to talk to someone about the confusion and turbulence appearing off and on in my life, my free-floating anxiety? What if I were to get the opinion of someone who I respect before I decide to act? What if I were to seek guidance from a doctor about taking medication to help me work through my late teen transition period? I wonder what my story might have been.

I am certain of this. On this trip, this journey, this saga of my life, I most definitely get my feet wet. The rocks I choose to cross the stream leave me far short of the other bank and I'm in the water, over my head. I suffer, but I don't drown. Was all of this necessary? Looking back, I don't believe so. Can you see a time in your life when you felt the pressure of being in a predicament and just wanting a way out? Do you see a better way you could work through it?

Yes, my enlistment in the Navy may be the days of the "Silent Service," but I should not be silent about my questions and concerns. Maybe if I were to ask more questions and speak up, there would be fewer clouds. Maybe I would find some of those clouds with silver linings. You just never know.

Second Thoughts

※

When I was in my teens, concerns revolved around parents divorcing, alcohol abuse, peer pressure, racism, and a media-produced fear of marijuana addiction. Along with some of these same problems, today's youth face challenges almost no one imagined even five years ago. Troops are returning home emotionally, mentally, and physically damaged due to ongoing wars. Climate Change is real and an existential (survival-endangering) crisis. Social media and the internet are misinforming people and creating distrust and hate. Covid 19 and its variants have killed around 1,000,000 Americans and may never completely disappear. While vaccinations offer hope, many people are not willing to be vaccinated, allowing the virus to not only continue, but to morph into different, often more virulent and contagious forms. Parents send their kids off to school, scared that one day a shooting may prevent them from returning home.

Every generation must go through some form of adapting to the problems of the times. But today, many young people may find themselves overwhelmed. Just as I did during my youth, many depressed young people must also find their way through their own dark clouds.

Everyone gets sad at times. That isn't depression. But there's a sadness, a feeling of anxiety affecting attitude and behavior which comes and goes for no identifiable reason over a long period of time. This is called "free-floating" anxiety (depression.) It's rather like getting Covid, recovering and then catching it again and again. Could this be something you are dealing with?

The desire to escape, which can be one symptom of depression, takes many forms. I choose taking naps and surfing instead of studying. Too often, I choose not to take the time to consider matters, but to make life-changing decisions impulsively. Without counsel, I make choices for immediate action and change. This postpones any success in working THROUGH my encounters.

Find your path. But before taking that first step, carefully look over those rocks which appear to form a way across the stream. Know the people you can turn to for advice or develop them now and then LISTEN to them. Think everything through. Don't figure you'll do everything on your own and wait to see how things work out. You're worthy and precious. You will discover where you can focus your talent so it will be appreciated as you discover a way through those clouds of life and allow the sun to shine for you once again.

※

You can reach out for help. SAMHSA (Substance Abuse and Mental Health Services Administration) has counselors available by phone 24/7 to help. The number is 800 662 HELP (4357), and the website is:

https://www.samhsa.gov/find-help/national-helpline.

Dropping In Deeper

1. Why was the Vietnam "War" not technically a war?

2. Why can't an auxiliary submarine submerge in stormy seas?

3. What is the setting of the story? What was one advantage for young men at that time if they decided to attend college right after high school?

4. What comes to his mind when the author is hiding from security personnel at the Greek Theater? What connection can you make to this in your own life?

5. What could the author have done so that he did not feel so overwhelmed by the requirements of being on a submarine?

6. From your mind's eye sketch the location where the author and his friends sit as they watch concerts OR the USS Baya when it returns from sea trials. Be sure to provide a caption.

7. What is the greatest fear the author faces in the story? Name one fear that concerns you a lot. You don't have to explain it.

8. Why does the author feel depressed at the time of the story? What are some similar concerns for the youth of the 1960s and those of today?

9. What connection can you make between what destroys the USS Thresher and what causes the author so much anguish and concern?

10. Do you believe "free-floating anxiety" is a condition in many of today's youth? Why or why not?

11. What is the definition of "camaraderie" as in "...that camaraderie, that feeling of shared purpose..."? Use it in a sentence.

Chapter 12: County Line

– *First Encounter With Death &*
Wisdom Resulting From Experience

Do you have a Special Place, aside from home, where things have happened to you that you'll just never ever forget? It could be school, but I'm going beyond that. I'm asking you to think of somewhere you go, or used to, that always generates a swell of memories for you, some experiences that make you smile and some that give you reason to pause.

I have one such special place. It's County Line Beach.

I'm a surfer in the early 1960s. County Line is not just any surf spot; it's my home surf spot. It's about eighteen miles north of Malibu just past the Los Angeles/Ventura County line on the Pacific Coast Highway (PCH). That's where it gets its name.

County Line is a privately owned, undeveloped beach, but

no one seems to know who owns it. There is no county maintenance or lifeguard or anything like that. It's situated at the southern tip of Ventura County in a rural, sparsely populated area, with only one sheriff, Pete, who patrols it occasionally. I remember him hanging out at the Country Store, a small grocery and diner just on the other side of the Coast Highway, during daytime hours.

I will never forget the view coming down the hill and seeing County Line for the first time. As you approach it from Malibu, from the south, the Coast Highway drops down a hill and for about one-quarter mile, runs along about fifteen feet above the sandy beach to the left. Rocks, boulders, and dirt fill in the slope from the road down to the sand. Surfers and beachgoers park along the highway and work their way down to the sand. To the right side, the east side of the road, is an almost vertical dirt and stone embankment, about 15 feet high, flat on top with open fields of brush and chaparral leading to small mountains in the distance. There are no structures until you reach the Country Store with its asphalt parking lot to the right side of the highway, and Jordan's, a tiny hamburger stand, with its tiny asphalt parking lot, to the left side of the highway. Jordan's perches on the bluff overlooking the ocean.

Just before Jordan's there's a flat dirt and pebble parking area with a steel guardrail about 20' above the ocean. A 3' by 2' rusted steel sign with punched-out lettering reading "NO ALCOHOL" sits on a post just behind the guardrail. No one knows who put that there. It has no other markings. Below is the rocky point where we love to surf, especially in winter when the waves get huge (for us) thanks to large northwest swells.

Dolly, in her late 50s, and her family, manage the Country Store. You have no doubt seen the place in movies and commercials. It's a popular motorcycle stop. One movie that stands out in my memory is "Point Break". In the future "The Country Store" will be renamed "Neptune's Net." Dolly's daughter, Patty, in her early 30s, assists her. Patty's teeth are all mottled. She tells me that when she was pregnant with her first child, she didn't get enough calcium in her diet, so the fetus, as it was developing, literally drew the calcium out of her teeth!

Sometimes when I have to head back home near closing time Patty allows me to store my 10' 1" surfboard under one of the pinball machines there. Once in a while she offers me a bit of leftover chili. At age 16, still looking for my first job, I'm "barely surviving" on my $2.00 a week allowance, so anything helps. The Country Store is a wonderful place to know. And it's a special part of County Line.

Since there's so little law enforcement around, County Line's popularity for kids goes far beyond its being a good surf spot. It's a party beach. Teens come from Los Angeles, especially the San Fernando Valley, and many keep fires going all night. There's lots of yelling and drinking, and some fighting, especially on weekends. There have even been stories of a few murders occurring. Because of this, most surfers prefer to sleep in their cars on the bluff or the store parking lot. The Valley partiers also leave their mess behind – especially beer cans and broken bottles, which become a hazard to those of us walking across the beach to paddle out early the next morning. Only the waves washing over the area at high tide clean up the mess. There is no county or state cleanup crew.

Let me describe the different surf breaks there so that you can appreciate the beach the way a surfer might. We have names for the different wave breaks at County Line. The sandy beach area to the south has its best surf in the summer and fall when the south swells generated by cyclones and hurricanes from New Zealand and Mexico dominate. The left-breaking waves can be best then.

At the north end, just 100 yards up, the small rocky kelp-covered point comes through best in the winter and spring when the northwest swells generated by huge storms in the Aleutian Islands area arrive. Perfect right-breaking waves, often moving through the kelp, present a vision that will likely be sketched in a surfer's notebook in class. Many surfers, however, prefer to avoid waves out there because it requires a special technique to paddle through and catch waves in the middle of a kelp bed.

Straight out about one-quarter mile from the sandy beach is a reef that sometimes has waves during good-sized swells. It's easy to spot that reef because it also has a kelp bed floating above it. The waves tend to peak up, break quickly and then flatten out, so there isn't much to them. We call it "The Bombora." It isn't often ridden. I paddled out there and surfed it only one time.

Just around the corner of the rocky point to the north is an occasionally great left-breaking wave, contrary to the usual right-breaking winter waves. If you catch one on a good-sized day it peels straight toward a small bridge spanning a tiny, dried-up creek running under the Pacific Coast Highway. The left break is so enticing you want to stay on that wave as long as you can. The problem is that it leads you, seductively, right into those rocks and boulders! If you ride in too far, the water suddenly sucks out and you're on them! We call that break "Lunchbox." I broke my board in half there once.

Over the years, County Line has provided millions of memories to thousands and thousands of surfers. Some of these recollections relate to the waves and epic surf days and sunsets; others are connected to other adventures and events of a particular day or night spent on the beach. There are those times spent over at the Country Store as a few of us, in dripping-wet trunks and cold as a well digger's knees, huddle around the gas wall heater just inside the entrance door. Then there are memories of events full of mischief, sometimes life-threatening, up at the parking areas on the bluff and across by the store. The highway crossing there, with cars constantly speeding by at seventy miles per hour, has its own tales of peril to relate. I have examples of all of these memories. They're a gift to me from County Line.

In one instance, there's this poor tourist who, just after a rainstorm, steps right on the ground at the base of one of the power poles that run along the bluff. He probably just wants to watch the waves. How is he to know the transformer up above is shorting out into the ground? He dies, electrocuted, right on that very spot. Each surf session we walk past the base of that power pole as we carry our surfboards down to the surf.

A few careless pedestrians don't make it across that highway, along with that "chicken crossing the road." Sometimes thieves, undoubtedly from the Valley, break into cars and steal car stereos while we're surfing. Then there's that girl in a bikini hitching a ride. Her destination is north towards Ventura. I'm headed home, driving south, with a couple of surf pals. All of a sudden, we decide it's a great time for a drive to Ventura!

I'm 16 and have a baby blue '56 Chevy panel truck, complete with mattress and Tijuana tuck 'n roll upholstery. It's perfect for overnight sleepovers at the beach. One evening, while the setting sun can partially blind a driver heading northbound on the Coast Highway, I am driving north from Malibu, on a raised stretch of road about a mile from my destination, County Line. Maybe I can catch a few waves before dark. My plan is to sleep over inside my panel truck-wagon so I can paddle out early the next morning. There's a rumor that a swell is coming tomorrow. No one really knows.

It's open road. The posted speed limit is sixty-five but there really isn't much law around, so who knows how fast I'm going? Telephone poles string along the left side of the road. They seem to whiz by like cars traveling in the opposite direction. I may be going a bit faster than I think.

Up ahead I'm coming upon the only other car traveling the same way, and it's in the right lane from me. This is a four-lane highway with open fields and then sparse, secluded homes, some overlooking the ocean, on my left. To my right is that familiar fifteen-foot-high vertical dirt and rock embankment which gradually eases down to allow an occasional road to appear. It then rises back up for a mile or so until another road pops into view.

Sometimes after it rains or there's a particularly strong wind, and often for no apparent reason, a rock or small boulder may let go from the hillside and roll onto the highway. It's just understood that this may be coastline, but it is also country, and a driver or motorcyclist must always be vigilant.

As I approach the other vehicle and am about to overtake it, I spot a rock, maybe a foot in diameter, sitting on the road 200 feet ahead right in that car's path! But the car just keeps on speeding along in that lane! Maybe it's that setting sun that obscures the view. But it's evident now there will be a collision.

I hit my brakes to avoid it all and marvel as the other car plows right into the rock. I don't see what happens to the rock, but the car goes out of control, swings right, and rumbles up onto the vertical embankment, rather like a race car on a specially designed high-banking turn…except this is more like…have you ever gone to a county fair and ridden a Whirl-a-Gig, the ride where you stand against a circular wall that spins, the floor drops down, and you stay pinned against the wall? This automobile stays up, driver's door facing the ground, bouncing its wheels along the rock and dirt embankment, for maybe 100 feet. It then comes careening down, somehow wobbling its way swerving right and left until straightening out back on the highway! The car then just continues traveling on! This really happens!

I speed up, pulling alongside the other auto, to check on the driver. What I see astounds me. It's a little old lady, both hands on the upper portion of the steering wheel, just driving as if nothing has happened. I yell, "Hey! You okay?", but mostly just motion for her to pull over so we can check any damage to the car, and to see if she really is all right. She obliges.

She slows down and steers onto the dirt roadside, now just about a mile north of the Country Store. I walk over to her, smell hot oil, and can now see it gushing from under her car, pooling up in the dirt by the front tire. The rock has blown apart her oil pan. It's dusk. I ask the obvious. She replies, "Well, I think so. I figured since I seemed to be okay and the car was still running, I might as well just keep on going."

She has to be in shock. The oil has stopped leaking and I see no real danger in what is soaking into the dirt. "Can you give me a number to call so we can get help?"

"Yes. Here's my son's number," she replies, as calm as a teacher handing out the results of a final exam. I drive back to the Country Store to the payphone there. Her son is quite grateful that I have called and arrives in about 30 minutes. She seems fine the whole time. It's amazing!

Another time…after the Country Store closes and it's quite dark, we surfers position our parked vans and station wagons on the lot into a circle, rather like covered wagons did long ago out on the prairie. Someone has an old barbecue set up in the middle for making dinner and a fire. One older surfer, Rusty, who's in his mid twenties and used to be a cook in the Navy, has a VW van and prepares amazing meals inside his van on a stove. The delicious aroma wafts over all of us and we're so jealous, but only he and the lucky guy who comes along with him get to partake. The rest of us, well, we gather around, some standing, some having the luxury of beach chairs, usually all of us still hungry, and tell tales of the day mixed in with some messing around.

In the dark of night some fellow in a car pulls in off the highway, about 20 feet outside our sacred circle of vans, and interrupts us. "How far is it to Oxnard?" he yells, just wanting to be sure he's headed in the right direction.

Ron is fooling around with some bottle rockets he bought in Tijuana. He's using the flames in the barbecue to ignite the rockets. Instead of shooting them into the sky, he has just discovered the fun of aiming them at targets on the ground, like a trash can on the lot or across the highway toward the ocean. The guy has his windows open as he makes his inquiry and Rick lights up another bottle rocket: "Ready. Aim. Fire!" I'll never forget that driver ducking just in time as the little flaming rocket jets right through his window and out the other side to the highway! The driver barrels out of there, tires screeching. We all laugh so hard. Not a thought do we give as to what could have gone wrong here. We return to our stories…just the perfect end to another surf day.

Or, there's this one… One barely dawn summer morning I wake up in my car after once again sleeping over on the Country Store parking lot. Someone is yelling, "There's an accident up the road!" Another guy and I start up our wagons and head north a couple of miles on Pacific Coast Highway (PCH) as it winds its way just above the ocean towards Ventura. Only boulders and about a twenty-foot height advantage protect the highway from the waves. We come around a bend and suddenly, there it is!

A fire truck and ambulance, red lights flashing, block a portion of the highway. There's only an occasional passing car at this time of the morning, and a couple of them are parked along the road as a small crowd stands at the edge looking down at the ocean. There is no beach, only the boulders and rocks leading into the water. We park just a bit away and run over to see what we can.

There's a sedan, flipped upside-down, almost completely submerged, just beyond the steep embankment. The car shifts a bit with each wave that washes over it. The waves slam into the boulders, sending spray up almost to where we're standing at the highway's edge.

Someone calls out, pointing, "There's one!"

I look out and see this poor fellow floating face down next to the car – with each wave he's getting dunked and inched closer to the rocks. His shirt is half torn-off and his pants are down to his knees – white underpants are still intact, contrasting with the blue water. His shoes are still tied. Moments later one wave manages to pick the victim up and carry him right into the jagged boulders. He bounces off a couple of them with a sickening "thud" and then, with each wave as his body rolls, scrapes, and jiggles over the barnacle-shielded boulders, it wedges, it nestles, into a crag between a couple of them. We watch as the waves mercilessly continue to pound, and amazingly, undress him, bit by bit, even including his shoes.

Several firemen and paramedics are standing with the crowd, evidently deciding on their next action. It's a tense scene.

Within five minutes the poor man is just down to his white briefs which are now down around his ankles.

Using ropes the rescue crew lowers a gray metal caged sled over the side while two of the men work their way down to the victim. It takes them about 15 minutes to grapple with his beaten, bloody, naked body and push and tug and nudge him into the apparatus so he can be lifted up to street level.

I'm positioned on the boulders now, about 10 feet from the sled as they pull it up to the highway's edge. I don't know how I managed to get here. I'm looking, I'm gawking, with fascination, at my first dead person. They have positioned him on his back. He's all mangled. His blood smears the gray steel conveyance. His stomach looks like he's pregnant - all bloated with seawater.

Just as the cage and its passenger reach the highway, someone in a less-excited, more stern voice announces, "There's another one."

It turns out that three Navy guys had been speeding along the curving highway in the dark just before dawn. Their car missed a turn and flew out into the ocean, landing upside down.

I turn away from the scene, climb up the rocks and slowly walk back to my car. I don't look back. In moments I'm making a U-turn and returning to County Line. I've lost track of my friend. I have no idea what he's doing. He's off my radar. I don't need to see this kind of thing again. Ever.

The whole event disturbs me profoundly. But you know what? I still go surfing that day. I sit out in the water with something new to ponder...how those guys were alive and thriving just a few hours earlier...and now they're gone - all because someone decides to drive too fast one early morning on one fateful day.

Over the years I will never forget the sights of that dark early morning. It is to affect the care I take in my driving and preclude any tendency to speed. A movie or TV show might portray an event such as this. But to see it in real life, to know that the casualties this day are someone's husband, father, son, brother or uncle with family members now left behind to suffer, causes me to be so thankful to be alive.

I am also grateful to know County Line at a time when I am so free to discover and explore each and every day, with so few worries of the World to distract me. County Line, with all the experiences and life lessons it teaches me, makes it, indeed, my Special Place.

Second Thoughts

※

Having a Special Place in your life gives you a starting point, a "reset button" you can fall back upon when you feel you've lost your way. Many of your perspectives on life connect to it in various ways. I discovered some of my independence and the preciousness of life at County Line, along with other lessons. Know your Special Place, treasure it, and think back upon it often.

Dropping In Deeper

1. What is the story's setting (year and location)?

2. What makes County Line Beach different from beaches or other recreation areas you know?

3. What happens in the story that relates to centrifugal force? Have you ever experienced centrifugal force?

4. What is the definition of "seductive" as in, "...leads you seductively right into the rocks..."? Use it in a sentence.

5. What danger lies in the way the surfer handles the bottle rockets?

6. In the bottle rocket incident, a group of guys is encouraging a pal to do something foolish. If this were a group of girls, would they be apt to act the same way? Why or why not?

7. How does this story/lesson affect you? Describe your feelings after reading it.

8. Sketch the old lady in her car as your mind's eye sees it OR the view the author describes coming down the hill to County Line. Describe your picture with a caption.

9. Why was the author so affected by the accident? Is that a good thing or bad? Explain.

10. Have you ever witnessed an event or accident that profoundly touched you? What was it? How did it affect you?

11. Lots of people don't live near the beach. But everyone can have a "County Line" of their own, whether it's a waterfall, pond, lake, mountain, sand dune area, open meadow or field, or a particular place in town where it's fun to hang out with friends. Name a special place of yours. What makes it so special for you?

Chapter 13: Crossing A Stream - *Handling Impulsiveness*

There are those who make things happen.
There are those who watch things happen.
There are those who wonder, "What happened?"
AND THERE ARE THOSE WHO DON'T KNOW ANYTHING
HAPPENED AT ALL!

I love chess, but stink when it comes to strategy. If nothing else, I lack the patience to work out a plan of attack. I just wanna play!

While hiking, do you ever come across a stream you want to cross and spot some rocks providing at least the beginning of a path to the other side? Do you venture out onto that first set of rocks, or do you take the time to check things out around the bend to see if there might be a better way? I tend to grab at the first opportunity that seems like it might work, and many times get stuck midstream and end up having to try another approach. Sometimes I get my shoes wet. Sometimes I make it. Sometimes I don't. It makes life interesting! It's how I've spent much of my time on this Planet.

Being this way means I may often miss something better, more appropriate, coming my way right around the corner, something that a more observant and disciplined person is more likely to find. Are you the type of person who takes the time to work out a strategy, an approach, or do you dive right in?

Now, think about how observant you are in your daily life. Are you fairly aware of what is taking place, or are you a bit oblivious - a bit too preoccupied with what you are doing to take notice of what else is happening?

Look over these four scenarios and see where you find yourself and your approach to living:

1. Here is an example of "making things happen" where the outcome is positive.

I'm in my late 30s. I'm one of only two male teachers at an elementary school. That means there are obligations for me that the female teachers don't have. I must always maintain a behavior and attitude beyond anyone's ability to suspect as inappropriate or questionable. For example, if a student returns alone to the classroom at lunchtime to retrieve a forgotten lunch bag, I must hold the door open and stand part-way in the hallway in full view of any passers-by until the child leaves the room. If I were a female teacher, it wouldn't be much of an issue. I make things happen safely because I'm aware and careful.

2. Here is an example of "watching things happen" :

When I first start teaching the elementary grades, I am told, "If you're not in the process of becoming an administrator three years after getting tenure (that is, having a permanent teaching position), something's wrong." At that time men are expected to move up into school administration. I choose to stay working with the children and parents as a classroom teacher for my career. I don't want to sit behind a desk as a school principal. I watch things happen for others over the years, as some teachers, both male and female, move on to higher-paying administrative positions.

3. In this next instance, I plod along happily wondering, "What happened?":

Remember that stream where I grab the first easy opportunity to cross? Now, I'm teaching at a school in a fairly wealthy neighborhood that, rightly so, receives less state and federal funding. Because we get less money from the government, that means our school has fewer regulations to follow than a school that does accept government funding. A problem with that is that there are few limits upon how many students a teacher can have. The only requirement is that we must follow what the fire marshal will allow. I have 36 students in my room, while other schools in less fortunate neighborhoods might only have 28. But I do have the advantage of strong parental support and involvement.

My classroom has old asbestos-lined tile flooring and no air conditioning, even though we are located in the hottest region of Los Angeles. Those schools in less fortunate neighborhoods boast carpet and air conditioning. It's so hot in my classroom that art projects in late spring and fall cannot include the use of crayons. Otherwise, students come to me with crumpled-up, melted crayons in hand, complaining, "I can't color the page. The crayon keeps smushing." The crayons are more like molding clay; paper sticks to the kids' arms when they raise their hands. It's rather humorous to watch. The whole scene might make great sit-com material, but it's real! That's how it is in these days.

Now that you have some background, here's the "What Happened?" story: It's Halloween. Each year I dress up as some kind of character. I've dressed up as Superman, with a costume homemade by my wife - red tablecloth for a cape; a large felt "S" pinned to my blue long-sleeved T-shirt; salad oil in my blonde hair to darken it a bit. This year, though, I'm not such a powerful character. She dresses me up as Pinocchio from the Walt Disney film.

She constructs a cute little brown felt hat and off-white felt nose, uses rouge to paint my cheeks with a little red circle on each, hangs a loose-fitting tie around my neck over a tightly fitting white T-shirt, and draws little black "rivets" on both sides of my knees. These are quite visible as I sport some really snug, popular-in-the-day, blue Ocean Pacific shorts which only reach half way down my thigh. Halloween is my favorite holiday of the year, so I'm happy to go along with it. I teach in this outfit the entire day of October 31 and participate in the Halloween parade which follows lunch.

I'm in the middle of presenting a lesson to my fifth-grade class that morning when the room speaker buzzes, "Mr. McBride, please come to the office." This is not a normal procedure at our school. Usually, a note is sent by the office to the classroom asking the teacher to drop by during lunch break or recess.

After a few moments of organizing my students, I open the door between classrooms, inform the other teacher that I have been summoned so she can "cover" my class, and out I scamper. I have no idea why I've been requested to appear in the office.

The principal's office door is wide open. His secretary gives me a curious look, although she has already seen my costume, and in I go. There is another adult seated in the room. Both the principal and the other gentleman there are in customary coats and ties. As I enter, the principal stands up, walks over and closes the door, and looks at me. "Mr. McBride, have a seat. This is Mr. Smith, Jane Smith's father." (Jane is one of my students).

I sense there is something wrong here. But what is it?

In a short time, I can see what is taking place.

Mr. Smith does not care for my method of discipline. He says Jane has complained to him about my requiring the class to march outside, silently in two lines, in perfect order.

This is a technique I learned when I was in the military. It worked on my fellow soldiers and me and has proven effective in settling down my students when they get too noisy or a bit uncooperative.

But lately, I've been a bit careless about using it. Normally, I walk with them or stand nearby, monitoring how quiet they are. But now when they are a bit unruly, I choose to put the class on "autopilot," having them march back and forth outside the classroom until they quiet down. I sit in the classroom, out of the hot sun, and watch. This is the situation to which Mr. Smith refers. As I now sit there in the principal's office, silently reflecting upon my behavior, I can't find much of any way to justify my actions.

So here I am, in my Pinocchio outfit, while a concerned parent in business attire brings up a perfectly legitimate complaint about my approach to discipline. I'm not in a good position.

Slowly, carefully, as the two of them are locked in conversation regarding how I may or may not have acted, I reach up and peel off my felt nose and lay it in my lap. Done.

They turn to inquire about what my intentions were by staying inside, but before I can explain anything, the principal makes another comment and Mr. Smith turns to respond to him. Now, I have my chance to slowly, carefully, take off my brown felt hat and also lay it on my lap. My hair isn't exactly in proper form, but so be it. Now that's done.

There's not much I can do about the red cheeks, the loose necktie, and painted-on knobby knees accentuated by my bright turquoise blue shorts. Oh well.

My class is back in Room 26 on their own "autopilot", doing a good job of cooperating. I have left enough to keep them occupied, and they really are a responsible group. I just wish I could tele-transport myself back to them, away from the situation I have created by being a bit lazy. However, I also realize Jane must know why I am in the office – and by now all the students are aware, as well.

Before I've really had the chance to say anything substantial, my principal offers this amazingly wonderful statement:

"I know Mr. McBride. He's a great teacher. He cares about his students. We all know how children can tell stories when they get home that may not be completely accurate. I'm sure there's a misunderstanding here. Mr. McBride will make certain everything is worked out and Jane will be fine."

Mr. Smith starts to say something but stops. The principal nods to him reassuringly. The two shake hands. I say a couple of words confirming that, of course, this is a misunderstanding. I say I will make certain that all will be well, shake Mr. Smith's hand, and the principal walks around from behind the desk and opens the door. With a wave, Mr. Smith heads out of the office.

My boss then closes the door while I remain.

There I stand, still in his office. My hair is definitely a mess. My red cheeks are a bit smeared at this point. The tie looks pretty straggly, and my shorts are way too short – knobby knees are looking pretty good, but they're a bit wobbly, as you can understand!

But I am feeling his support. I'm feeling he believes in me as one of his top teachers. I'm feeling... "Pete! What the hell happened!?"

I respond, "Well, I was just being consistent in trying to enforce …"

"That guy is a Philadelphia attorney! He came here ready to sue you and the district for what went on with that marching and everything! You have to promise me whatever you did will not happen again! Do you understand!?"

My left hand reaches up and squeezes my cheeks and chin. I hope I'm looking thoughtful, as thoughtful as a fellow half-made up as Pinocchio can appear.

"Yes sir!" I respond.

He opens the door for me. The office manager gives me a little bit of a comforting smile.

I head to the bathroom. I can't get that darned red off my cheeks without a shower. I have no other clothes for changing. So, I turn myself back into Pinocchio and march back to good ol' Room 26 shaking my head wondering, "What happened? There I was, teaching away when suddenly I'm called to the office, almost lose my job, and I could have been sued!"

I must compose myself to again be their teacher. I manage,

but under the phony felt nose, my real nose has grown a bit longer now because I wasn't totally truthful. I do learn a lesson, though. If I use my marching technique, I use it carefully and caringly from now on!

This whole incident blows over and fades into the parade of my career memories. My principal believes in and supports his faculty members. I love him for letting me learn and for not having me suffer too much from my mistake.

My shoes get wet in the stream, but I don't fall in …this time.

4. This incident involves me "not being aware that anything has happened at all". I never see this coming:

In order to assist with an additional fifth grade class, the following year the principal hires an experienced teacher with whom he is familiar. At our first meeting with her on faculty he explains, "She's a wonderful teacher! She came out of retirement to be a member of our faculty, and I appreciate her doing so!"

A couple of months down the line she and I happen to be standing together in the school office. I'm reading a note I've just retrieved from my teacher's mailbox. She turns to me and comments, "Peter, remember there is a meeting after school."

I know she means to be helpful. I appreciate her caring enough about me to be sure I know about the meeting. I understand all of this. But I make a careless response. I'm going through my mail, not really concentrating upon what she has said. So, just like your leg juts forward when the doctor hammers on your knee, I reflexively mumble, "It's okay. You don't have to nag me. I'll be there."

She's startled! She's insulted! "What?! I've been married 32 years and my husband has NEVER EVER called me a nag!"

I respond, "Oh, I'm sorry. I didn't mean it that way. Honest."

We part and attend the meeting and life goes on.

I don't realize anything has happened! But it has. Oh, I do notice that she does not talk to me much anymore unless it's because we're both teaching fifth grade and we must discuss an issue related to our classrooms. I just attribute that to her being very busy and focused. But I find out later that she has opposed every project or activity I have promoted for the school. Her criticism of me probably still echoes in the hallways. I miss out on understanding that she truly dislikes me. That incident has been our only meaningful interaction, and it has sealed my fate with her.

It's so important to measure our words, especially when we're speaking to those who we do not know well. A careless or casual comment can be misunderstood. It makes it that much harder to find the right rocks to tread upon in order to reach the other side of the stream.

Second Thoughts

※

We all find adventures in life. Some we cause to happen. Some just occur on their own. Some we just cannot understand how they happened. And some take place without our even realizing it until it's too late.

The gift that an excellent teacher, religious leader, family member, friend, colleague, or boss can provide is to give patient guidance – through suggestions or observations, not just commands. We look for those rocks we can spot and step upon in order to make it across, wherever and whatever they may be. We can help others find their own rocks, their paths, as well. But we need to know when to step back and let them explore the rest of the way on their own. It may require them more than one attempt. Exploration is essential to living a productive life. Sometimes, we get our feet wet in the process.

Dropping In Deeper

1. Why is the author embarrassed when he enters his principal's office?

2. If you, without thinking, blurted out, "You don't have to nag me," in a similar situation, (maybe with your mom or a friend), what steps can you take to help that person not have their feelings hurt?

3. Describe a time when you have acted before thinking it through. What was the outcome? How did you manage to make it right? Or did you not?

4. From the female teacher's view, why does she take offense to the author's "nag" comment? Would you? Why or why not?

5. How would you help a friend avoid a mistake you know is coming as a result of the circumstances?

6. So, which one are you? Do you start across those rocks in the stream without being certain they connect to the other side... or do you take the time to check around the bend to see if there is a better crossing over there? Tell about an event from your life which demonstrates which of these descriptions pertains to you.

7. What does the word "oblivious" mean, as in "...are you a bit

oblivious...?" Use it in a sentence.

8. Sketch the stream you're hoping to cross as your mind's eye sees it OR a picture of the author sitting in the principal's office. Describe your picture with a caption.

Chapter 14: Social Experiment - *Race Relations & The Problem With Good Intentions*

This is a tough story to write. "No way,"" you may respond. "You've written about movies that frighten you so much you can't sleep two years later. You relive your first encounter seeing somebody die a violent death. You describe being on the wrong side of a love triangle and getting tossed out the door. How can there be a tougher story for you to write? "

I get hurt in this one. Physically. Severely. There's no happy ending. I'm like a toddler who explores the World by reaching on the top of the table, the chair, and then eventually the stove with the front burner lit. I put my little hand into the flames – except now I'm 22 and the stove top is a summer festival in a distant neighborhood. OK, here goes.

As a little boy I lived in rural Georgia in the early 1950s. I was in the first grade of an all-white school. Black children had to ride a bus to another school on the outskirts of our town. I was too young back then to be aware of the policies of segregation with its separate schools, bathrooms, and drinking fountains for Blacks. (You may or may not learn about this in school, but it's a part of our American history you should know.)

At my school we didn't have enough textbooks, so we shared, and some of the other white schools in our area didn't even have enough desks, so pupils had to sit together in pairs! I remember seeing billboards with pictures of students sharing desks, encouraging people to vote for a school bond. Many people lived in poverty in the community, including my own white schoolmates. Yet, conditions for Black people were much worse. Their school was much worse, as well.

One autumn day when my dad drove me to school, I sat in the back seat so he couldn't see that I was barefoot. I wanted to go barefoot like some of the kids in my class were allowed to do. He didn't see my feet when I climbed out of the car, and all went well until the teacher noticed and called home for my mom to bring my shoes. I looked on it as a special treat to go barefoot, but Mom later told me that these children came to school that way because they didn't own shoes. "There's little money for the schools and the families of the poor only get what they can for doing odd jobs," she would say. As an adult I would realize that in Georgia in those days there was no safety net like unemployment assistance or food stamps for the general population. Poorer families had to rely upon churches and community donations for survival.

For those who were Black, conditions were terrible. The government made very little effort to even provide them with an education. It was believed, though not stated publicly, that by keeping Blacks ignorant of anything they might be entitled to –

through laws and policies -- they could be "handled" more easily. Sadly, that manipulation meant Blacks could be paid very little while performing the critical tasks of tending to the crops, serving in white people's homes as babysitters and handymen, and working as poorly paid cooks and maids.

People in the Black community had few rights; this abuse by the white majority never made a headline. Blacks were even denied access to the voting booth. Technically, they did have the right to vote, but they were required to pass literacy tests and/or recite the entire U.S. Constitution – all devious, sneaky ways to keep Blacks from casting their ballots. That policy of keeping them from voting continues in Georgia to this day. Civil rights groups are in court and in congressmen's offices working to change these ways. Yet, at this writing, opposing political forces are also at work in many states attempting to pass laws to limit who can vote and their ability to cast their ballots.

We moved from Georgia to Philadelphia when I was six and then on to Los Angeles when I was nine. In later years, as a teacher in Los Angeles, I met a Black colleague who coincidentally grew up in that Georgia town at the same time I did! I discovered what Blacks had to endure back then. This would become part of my impetus, my inspiration, for wanting to go to Watts, a predominantly Black neighborhood of Los Angeles, to share in its summer festival.

The Watts Riots had taken place there in 1966 – a time when on a hot summer night, some Blacks -- frustrated with their poverty, lack of jobs, poorly supported schools, and unfair treatment by police in Los Angeles -- began looting stores and setting buildings on fire. Certainly there were those who were opportunists, just taking advantage of the chaos and stealing. It started because of the way a Black male was treated by police while being arrested for drunk driving. To appreciate how bad things were, consider that the L.A. Police Chief William H.

Parker publicly called the Watts rioters "monkeys in the zoo."

Now it's 1972. There's the feeling in the white community that things are improving for the Black community – a lot of us, especially those of us in college and those who believe that "All men (and women) are created equal," are reaching out to help in our own ways. This is also the era of "Free Love" which came into prominence in San Francisco in the 1960s. Civil rights and loving one another are "in the air."

Having served in the Navy, I've already crossed the Pacific Ocean and been to Vietnam, the Philippines, Hong Kong, and Japan. There have been some close calls, but I've come through without injury. I know how to look out for myself.

The Watts Summer Festival takes place for a weekend each summer in the middle of that primarily Black region on the south side of Los Angeles. The festival is a celebration of Black culture, history and social and political progress. Booths are set up to display and sell ethnic art, clothing, music, and food; carnival rides, like a Ferris wheel, attract adults and children. About 100,000 attend the festival over that weekend. It's well organized and a big deal.

My major in college is cultural anthropology (the study of human societies and cultures) and, after reading a newspaper article about the event, I decide this sounds like a great opportunity, a kind of a "social experiment" as I call it, to meet and greet and share with those in the Black community!

I call a major Los Angeles newspaper to pose the question, "Will white people be welcome at the Watts Festival?"

These fateful words are spoken in response, "Of course! You'll have a great time!"

My girlfriend, who is in my sociology class, expresses her enthusiasm as well. She'll go, so I call my brother, two years my junior, and invite him and his girlfriend. I'll never forget his wary, "What?! What are you thinking? That's no place for us!"

But I believe it is. We're living in an era of change. I'm fairly good at convincing people and he gives in, so early the following Saturday afternoon we're on our way to Watts to participate in the festival.

Though I've lived in Los Angeles since I was nine, I need directions in order to find that neighborhood. We park a few blocks away from the large open grass park where the festival takes place and we approach the grounds. There are some trees surrounding the area, but not many. Have I considered that we probably won't see any other whites there except for a few of the guys' girlfriends? No. It's rather daunting to walk into an unknown place with thousands and thousands of people who look different. I remember my brother remarking, "This isn't a good idea."

"Oh, we'll be fine," I reply in my wisest sage voice. I don't want the girls to get upset. I certainly don't want anyone to think I'm mistaken. My belief is that if we all have the right attitude, things will work out great.

Did you ever go someplace where you're different in some way from everyone else? Maybe you've attended a school where you are the only student of a particular ethnicity. Maybe you've been invited to attend a wedding or religious service where your religious or cultural background is different. Perhaps you're the only female working in an office of men or the only girl at a meeting. Then you know how things are looking to us about now. We're not accustomed to feeling this way: uncomfortable, that is, out of place. I begin to appreciate the strain People of Color must often experience and accept as just part of going through any normal day – everyday, for some.

We walk through the trees and enter the park, thick with people. It reminds me of working my way through the crowd at a Los Angeles Dodgers game. My brother and I are holding tightly onto our girlfriends' hands. There's unfamiliar music playing, and voices are everywhere. So far, so good. We meander around and a lot of people smile at us. We ride the Ferris wheel and taste the food.

A guy approaches and claims, " I'm from the African Methodist Episcopal Church. How about giving a donation?" As I'm thinking about how to respond, a number of people gather to watch how I answer his request. I ask, "Do you have any identification or anything?"

"F--- you!" and he stomps away. But really, that's the only difficult moment of our several hours there. He never returns and no one else approaches us like that again.

We've spent a couple of hours and a little money and it's getting into the late part of the afternoon, and we all agree it's time to leave. It's been one of those experiences you look forward to recalling sometime as you begin, "I remember the time…" We have no idea of the encounter ahead of us.

All of those thousands and thousands of people have been quite accepting of us. We, likewise, have been very accepting of them. No one is giving the "stink eye" or anything like that. We've had a good time, and I'm rather proud of my social experiment and the way we make it work.

As the four of us approach the trees at the perimeter of the park, the girls walking and talking together in front of my brother and me, there's a stir. A fellow in the crowd, a really big guy, walks over and puts his arm around my brother's girlfriend. He says,

"She's going with me."

My brother tells him, "I'm sorry. She's with me."

In the flash of a second the culprit turns towards us and takes an unexpected swing at my brother's head and connects. I'm seeing all of this happen in the space of five seconds. My brother hits the grass, rolls, and struggles up. He stands there, dazed, after that sucker punch. Now there's a crowd, and the background noise shifts to loud yelling and whooping. "Don't hit me!" some taunt my brother. He says nothing. He's frightened for his life.

A few of the women yell, "Leave him alone!" in an attempt to halt the ensuing slaughter. Maybe they have seen too much of this sort of thing – one man beating up on another. In contrast, most of the fights I've ever witnessed have ended up with the guys becoming buddies afterwards!

Not here. Not now. This is my "social experiment" with variables I have not anticipated or allowed for. The result of my experiment could be deadly.

The mass of people now forms a circle around all four of us. From up above it must appear like a large boxing ring, except there will be no boxing at this event. It's a no-holds-barred Ultimate Fighting arena where the contestants are a ridiculous mismatch. The guy looks like an NFL tackle.

The assailant, hands raised for another punch, again advances toward my brother. At the same time, a guy comes up behind my brother's legs and drops to a push-up position waiting for him to step back and fall. Then something takes place which seals my fate in all of this.

The big guy goes for the second wallop, but as he does, my brother, instead of stepping back, instinctively dodges to one side. That flying fist finds air and then plummets into the grass as the guy trips over the fellow in push-up position. It's a bit humorous to watch for the first three seconds, except you can't keep a bad guy down.

My brother sails out of there, breaks through the ring of people, and hightails it into the park with the embarrassed and furious lug behind him. It looks to me like, unimpeded, my brother can out-distance the huge guy. Now, it's my turn to participate in my "experiment." That's not what I think consciously; it's just what I do.

I look over at the shocked girls, standing next to one another, and tell them, "Stay together!" With no strategy, no plan, I start running along the path of parted people created by my brother and his pursuant as I yell, "That's my brother! That's my brother!"

It's the last thing I will recall as the next ten minutes of my life vaporize from my memory. Even today I can remember only tiny snippets of what occurs.

I'm 170 pounds and athletic. I've played as a guard on my high school football team. I've had a few fights here and there in my time, especially on the sand and in the water at the beach over somebody taking my waves when I'm surfing – silly stuff. I've been the "victor" meaning, they don't take my waves anymore. I can't recall anyone ever getting even a bloody lip in my fights. And, as I say, I've traveled around the World thanks to Uncle Sam.

But now, I'm in the wrong place at the wrong time, quite out of my league.

I don't know where this guy comes from, but I know how he finds me – he hears me yelling, "That's my brother! That's my brother!" somewhere from behind. He decides to drop out of the chase and here I come, right to him! As I say, I have no recollection of the first punch – or the last, but just little instances.

The guy changes targets, and I'm the bullseye now. The next thing I remember, I'm backed up against a small grandstand, bleeding profusely from my face. I keep pleading, "I don't want to fight. I don't want to fight." He moves in for the kill.

You wonder, wouldn't it be ironic if he were from Georgia or the South? Maybe I'm witnessing the end result of another "social experiment," that of his mistreatment by the whites where he grew up or the mostly white police force, there or here in Los Angeles. He could be so full of hate and anger at the system and his surroundings that he just can't help taking it out on something – or someone. And here I am.

A Black guy beats up a white guy, yes. But how many times have the players been reversed? How many times have whites, including local police, ganged up on Blacks over the centuries of U.S. history? How many "knees to the neck" have they suffered? How many times has a white guy, brandishing a gun, found himself restrained and then arrested by the police, whereas a Black guy, wielding a knife or no weapon, loses his life to police gunfire?

My experiment has failed to take into consideration the historic and monumental force of racist abuse vs. the pitiful nudge of my good intentions. I'm at the wrong end of the scale, receiving the brunt of this guy's anger. I'm the little kid on a seesaw when a bully unexpectedly jumps on the opposite end and bucks her up into the air. She then finds herself plummeting to a crash-landing on the ground.

I don't remember how it happens, but I'm on the ground now.

More blood pulses from the side of my face and drips from inside my mouth, but strangely, I'm numb to the pain. I've never known this feeling before. Clearly, I'm hurt, but there's no feeling or sensation, just the awareness of my own blood all over me.

I don't know what has happened to my brother or the girls. There's that circle forming again. I'm in the arena and I'm the main draw, no doubt. I'm aware of some voices calling, "Aw come on!" as if they have seen enough and the guy should stop. But others just yell, like the thousands of fans do at an Ultimate Fighting match. Here, however, there's no referee to intervene and wave off the opponent.

He attacks again.

That's all I know. That's all I can visualize. My next clear moment comes when I regain consciousness as someone rubs my left wrist and hand. It's a female sheriff. I'm on my back. Blood is what I know now. I feel it soaking my hair, my neck, my shirt. There's some kind of pain, I don't know, coming from under my right eye. My mouth is all swollen and my lips...Have you ever accidentally bitten your lip and that little piece of lip tissue just rests inside your mouth a day or so until it heals? Imagine doing that over and over and over again so the whole mouth feels like it's shredded. That's how my lips feel right now as I taste lots and lots of blood.

The rest of my body, my groin, my side, my legs, are numb. I can still move, I'm not paralyzed, but I'm unaware of any kind of specific pain from those areas.

I'm in shock. I remember studying about it in a Red Cross class a few years prior. My body is shutting down to some degree in order to protect itself – like when your phone battery is almost dead, and the phone goes into "standby" mode. I'm aware they're putting me on a gurney and sliding me into an ambulance. I think I fall asleep because I can't remember the ride. I don't even know if they sound the siren! But as the paramedics wheel me to the procedure room of the emergency ward of the hospital, I do recall the ceiling lights parading by overhead.

Meanwhile, back at the park, as the sheriffs arrive, my brother manages to circle back to the girls. Neither he nor the girls see me, but a sheriff informs them of my ambulance ride. There's uncertainty as to which hospital I'm heading to and what will happen next. They've all been through enough trauma for one day and my brother takes them home and informs my parents.

The next thing I know I'm in a regular room in the hospital and my dad is by me.

The assailant has vented his hate upon me. His kicks have landed everywhere – lower extremities to just under the right eye. The curved front of his shoe has torn apart the skin lying on the bone at the bottom of my eye socket, creating a curved scar that will last me a lifetime. While the shoe has also hit my eyeball, it's not enough to burst it – just enough to turn the whole eye cherry-red for months. I would have issues with eye pressure in that eye for the rest of my life.

Had he landed his kick upon my temple that hard…I might not be here today.

The inside of my mouth, especially in the lip region, requires so many stitches that when it heals, my lips are altered enough to change my smile forever. I choose to sport a mustache to camouflage the damage and do so to this very day.

A couple of days later, as I'm home recovering, I call the sheriff's station and discover they managed to arrest the guy! I've thought about the whole incident, and I don't want him just to walk away without consequences. Otherwise, he's encouraged to do it again to someone! They tell me he was under the influence of something, probably alcohol. They also tell me, after being held in jail two nights, he was released. If I want to follow up on this, I must take all four of us back to Watts, to the sheriff's station to fill out a report. I'm told we can't go to a different station closer to home. When I start to question this, the sheriff curtly cuts me off saying, "You had no business being there." I can visualize him shaking his head.

The possible consequences, and certainly the distress, of the four of us returning to Watts are too great. This "experiment" has to end. Now. I never even discuss or write about this event in my sociology class. It's just too painful.

Sadly, if you followed the events of 2020, including the nationwide news story about the murder of a Black man, George Floyd, by the police in Minneapolis, you'll see that these battles are still being fought. It would seem Democracy in the U.S. is still in the "experimental" stage.

Second Thoughts

※

At the end of an experiment, a scientist weighs the results and draws conclusions. Mine are stated in the form of "Lessons". See if these make sense to you. They come from experience. Mine.

Conclusion (Lesson) 1: People of Color may often be under strain and stress every day when they live or work in a predominantly white neighborhood in the United States.

Conclusion (Lesson) 2: Though there may be thousands of law-

abiding people at an event, it only takes one person's actions to ruin the day for others. In my case it is one violent man. It could have just as easily been one person with a gun. On the road it could be one drunken driver. This is an amazing display of the influence and power just one person's behavior can have upon the lives of so many others.

Conclusion (Lesson) 3: My mom always said, "The road to hell is paved with good intentions." Certainly, my intentions in initiating this day at the festival were good, but they were naive. Just having genuinely worthy reasons for doing something does not guarantee things will work out for the best. We have to weigh the need vs. possible consequences and what we can actually count upon accomplishing.

Conclusion (Lesson) 4: Over the history of the United States, there have been so many instances of discrimination against what white supremacists regard as "immigrants" or "outsiders." An incomplete list includes the Native Americans, Chinese, Jews, Irish, Polish, Italians, Russians, Japanese, Latinos, Hispanics, and on and on. American hate groups presently focus upon Latinos, Blacks, Jews and Asians. Former President Trump made unsubstantiated statements blaming China for creating Covid-19, providing even more raging fuel for racial tension across the country.

Conclusion (Lesson) 5: One person or group of a particular ethnicity or profession harming others does not mean that everyone of that culture or occupation does this or believes in such behavior. You cannot make that assumption. It is a mistake to hold everyone in a group accountable for one person's actions. It is a mistake to hate. While some police officers abuse their power, most do not. It was just one man who attacked the author while thousands of others had been quite accepting of him, his brother, and their girlfriends.

Conclusion (Lesson) 6: It is important to understand that everyone around you has had different experiences in life. They don't necessarily see the World as you do. Keep in mind where you are and your surroundings and know that some may harbor resentments against you just for your appearance or how you talk. Find your best way to cope with this and be careful, but remember to balance everything with the potential joy of meeting others and exploring new places.

Dropping In Deeper

1. What is one example of the poverty the author becomes aware of as a child in Georgia in the early 1950s?

2. The author speaks of the sensation of feeling out-of-place and uncomfortable because of his being different from the other people at the festival. Describe a situation where you have felt this way.

3. Why does the author wish to attend the Watts Summer Festival?

4. This is a difficult, disturbing story. Can you find some form of hope in its message? What would that be?

5. Describe a time when someone does not understand or appreciate something the way you do. It could be as simple as a movie or TV show you watch together. Or it could be something you do with good intentions, but someone misunderstands and doesn't like.

6. From your mind's eye, sketch a picture of the Watts Summer Festival as the author and group first approach it OR the situation you describe in question #5. Include a caption which describes your picture.

7. How old is the author when he attends the festival? Do you

think he would have done the same thing if he were five years older? Why or why not?

8. What is the meaning of "variables" as in "...with variables I have not anticipated..."? What are two variables the author fails to consider in his "social experiment"?

9. Choose one of the Conclusions (Lessons) which makes sense to you and would be your favorite. Why do you choose this one?

Chapter 15: Luck Wears A Veil - *The Roles Of Luck & Impulsiveness In Our Lives*

I t's part of being a boy, I think. Many of us find fascination in seeing something dead or in killing things, like insects. It may be squashing anthills or spiders. It may be staring at a dead mouse in a mousetrap. I guess girls can go through this, too, but it does feel like this is part of our natural male development, some phase. Possibly it's the hunter instinct in us.

For my thirteenth birthday, my parents have gifted me with a Ben Pearson 30 lb. fiberglass recurve bow! Yes, it's to shoot real arrows! It's beautiful, sporting a brown plastic grip in the middle with a small ledge on top for the arrow to sit upon, and the rest all yellow fiberglass. With it comes a brown leather quiver which includes a strap running from shoulder to hip so the pack settles in against my upper back – I can easily reach over my shoulder for any of my precious five arrows. I am Robin Hood!

There's a park not too far away with an archery range consisting of five bales of hay for target practice and an empty wooded area behind it…in case you miss. My neighborhood friend, Mike, and I enjoy the mile hike up to the field most Saturday mornings. It's perfect.

I'm not a great shot and I spend a good deal of time looking for my lost arrows in the woods. I'm proud of myself for being wise and careful enough to stay out of range of the other archers. I'm very aware that back in those woods, a distracted moment, even just getting distracted by a squirrel, could instead mean another archer's unintended arrow in my back.

But there must be something more than just shooting at an already tattered paper target, right? I'm thinking this one crisp blue sky summer morning as Mike and I walk home from a session at the archery range. We're trodding along the 20' wide grass median that separates the two one-way access roads which meander through the residential area just below the park. We've just strolled by a groundskeeper who crouches beside a sprinkler head he's replacing.

It's wonderful with all of the bright sunshine and soft grass, and things are so very quiet because at that moment there aren't any cars passing by. I look up to see a bird flapping its wings close enough. This triggers something in a primitive section of my brain, and I instinctively reach back, grab an arrow, swiftly set its notch in my bow string (maybe you have seen this maneuver in "The Hunger Games"), arch back and let the arrow fly at the bird – straight up at this point. I miss. Darn it.

You know what an arrow does when it goes straight up in the air? Yup, it comes straight down – well, almost.

As Mike and I strain our eyes looking upward, hands covering our eyes from the sun to try and spot where the arrow flew, we know the bird has already escaped. But the arrow, well, it's disappeared! It's out of sight! I mean, it's like something out of "The Twilight Zone." The sky has swallowed it up! I know I launched that arrow with all my might, but how could it just go away? It's just gone…it's just…

The quiet of the morning is shattered by the piercing sound of, "Hey! You kids!" It startles us. We both simultaneously turn to the source and see that the crouching groundskeeper, maybe 20' away, now stands, and about a foot and a half from his left shoe rests my arrow – sunken half its length into the grass! It's as if I was just sitting in a tree above the guy, shooting an arrow right at him and just missing! I gain my first truly appreciated experience of a law of physics --- you know, what goes up must come down – and it comes down just as fast as it goes up! The same principle works for bullets fired into the air. They don't drift down to the ground. Bullets come firing back to the ground with the force that sent them up. It's really dangerous!

We don't waste a second, though, thinking these deep thoughts; they will come to us at a later time. Away we scatter, pell-mell, Mike down one side of the median and me down the other, as fast as our four little legs can carry us, heading for home. We don't look back for a long time. But a few minutes later we stop to take a peak. All clear. The park road has now become the boulevard which passes by home. The groundskeeper has become a thing of the past.

I shake my head. Mike yells, "That was really dumb!" Maybe he's a little upset, but he's also grinning at the whole situation. I really regret the stupidity of shooting my bow that way. Not only did I miss and not hit the bird, but it also cost me one of my bitchin' arrows! Of all the luck.

A couple of months later I'm off on a new adventure. Steve, another friend of mine, whose family owns not only a lovely home, but a horse ranch out in the country, invites me to go duck hunting with him. This is something I've never ever thought about doing, but I go along. His mom drives us to a club which offers potential members the opportunity to shoot at flocks of ducks trained to fly over a man-made lake.

The club sets us in a camouflaged blind overlooking that small lake. At the signal, the fowl are let go, and they dutifully fly across the middle of the lake right in front of us. Steve and I fire away with our 20-gauge shotguns – I shoot into the flock and with a little luck hit one and down it goes. A trained retriever swims out and snags the dead duck in its mouth and brings it right back to us!

This isn't the end of the story. The club charges $10 per duck – which is equivalent to $85 in today's money! And I must take the carcass back to Steve's home, pluck out all its feathers and the dark quill feathers beneath the skin. After that, tweezers in hand, I must extract every single piece of buckshot in the poor duck's body. What a hassle!

Oh, as an added "treat," Steve's brother goes to a pond that same day and shoots a couple of frogs. Along with the buckshot in the duck, I'm also carving out buckshot in frogs' legs! Whew! We have the frogs' legs and duck for dinner that night. It all tastes pretty good, but there's too much work involved! Steve's mom decides not to join the duck-hunting club.

All of this shooting and killing does not phase me at all. It's just part of the adventure of being a boy. Then, one summer day a few months down the road, things suddenly change.

Mike owns a BB gun, a kind of air gun that shoots small metallic balls and looks like a real rifle. He stores it behind the couch in their living room. I so want one, but Dad says, "No!" My thirteen-year-old brain can't understand his reasoning. It matters not. I won't be getting one.

That day Mike and I are messing around along the boulevard in front of his house. He has the BB gun, and, for some reason, he aims it at me! I'm not going to take the time to ask why; I just peel out, streaking up the grass adjacent to the sidewalk towards the shelter of home and make it about 50 feet before he fires.

There's a "thunk" sound of the pellet hitting my shirt and back, stinging and startling me. I'm writhing in pain - I think. Down I go, kind of like that duck I shot. Mike runs up, gun in hand, laughing. "Oh, quit acting!" he quips. After a little bit I realize I'm not dying. It just sort of hurts. I can live with that, but not his shooting at me!

"You rat. You shot me in the back!" We exchange insults, as boys do, and I win! By that I mean he feels a bit guilty, enough to loan me his rifle for a day to make up for the damage done.

I head home, BB gun in hand, entering by the backyard gate. I'm feeling that "hunter" urge again. I imagine I look like a soldier returning from war or frontiersman Davey Crockett coming back from a hunt in the woods. Our dog, George, stands just inside the glass-paned back door barking, "Hello!" as I pass by about twenty feet distant. I can sort of see him through the screen in front of it. Like days of yore with the arrow and the bird, I whirl around and without hesitating, impulsively fire a shot at the dog – which means at the screen – oh, and the glass door. There's a "thunk" which tells me I hit something. I figure the BB only stung me, so it will simply bounce off the screen, or if it gets through, at worst it will hit the glass and bounce off that.

Nothing much happens. George disappears but there's no whimper, so I know he's okay, just maybe a bit startled. As for everything else, well… I go and inspect. There's a hole in the screen. But maybe no one will notice. Upon a more thorough examination I must admit there is a bit of a hole in the glass pane as well. Evidently the BB doesn't just bounce off as harmlessly as I believe.

Interestingly, along with the BB-sized hole, now the glass has a very small cone-shaped gouge in it, with the widening of the cone facing outside. Up close it's a pretty design. Fortunately, this is a minor injury to the glass on the door, down in the lower right corner. No one will probably even notice it. That's a relief. Looks like I'm lucky on this one! Whew!

Not a soul is around. Upstairs, brandishing the BB gun still, I hustle to the guest room, which has a small balcony just outside. Once out there I look over and see, maybe three houses away in the bright sunshine, Mike's bedroom window. Of course, I fire off a couple of carefully aimed shots in that direction. No luck. There's no rewarding "thunk," just a disappointing silence. I know the BB gun can't really shoot that far, but it's fun to try! And there's no real danger of breaking anything. It's only when I aim for a palm tree just fifty feet away that I can hear the rewarding sound of a BB hitting a tree trunk. Ah, that keeps me occupied for a few minutes.

There's a tall pine tree nearby and, as I inspect, I spot the prize. I recall when that bird flew by overhead and it cost me an arrow. Here it is again! Ok, so maybe it's not the same bird, but it is the same opportunity, only it won't cost me an arrow this time. I have Mike's BB gun! Hidden amid green pine branches and bramble my prey just sits quietly on a limb or something. It's not easy to spot, but from this upstairs vantage point I have a better view than from down on the ground.

Now, I know the chances of hitting it are truly obscure. The little bird is a good distance away, tucked in the branches, and I'm not good at aiming Mike's BB gun with any accuracy. But there are other trees behind this one, so the BB won't accidentally do any damage to anything. If I were to hit my target it would be totally by luck.

I want to freeze frame this scene, with the bird in the gun site of Mike's rifle, to explain something about "luck." Luck wears a veil, and you can't always know what's behind it. Sometimes what seems to be good luck turns out to be bad luck – and vice versa. We know the term "dumb luck" comes from somewhere. Think of the sad stories of those who have won the lottery only to have misfortune overwhelm them afterwards – family strife, loss of friends, and loss of money.

I know I'm delaying the climax of the story here but again, I want you, the reader, to understand how luck can camouflage itself at times.

A few months before the BB gun and the bird, luck comes my way while I'm with my pal, John. He and I are fooling around on the dirt road of a new hillside development being built near his house just above the residential boulevard. The road, which rises steeply, is at that time just leveled off dirt and rock and on both sides there are bulldozed embankments with plateaus at the top for the homes yet to be built. There are unpaved streets branching off, all at this point, perfect for playing around. Nothing is being built now. We hike way up this quarter mile of dirt to the very top of the hill. It's a weekend, so nobody is working. The road even curves a bit half-way down, but you can still see and faintly hear the cars whizzing along below.

There's an old car tire somebody dumped off lying nearby. I halfthinkingly pick it up and give it a shove – just to see what it will do. I'm hoping with a little luck it will gain some momentum and crash into one of the dirt embankments nearby. Even if it were to roll down a bit, I'm certain it will bounce up one of the hillsides as the bumpy dirt road makes its turn. There's little chance it will go anywhere.

The tire takes off, wobbles at first almost lying out flat, but then picks up speed and starts down the road. It swerves to one side and the other, bouncing as it goes, hits the curved section rolling right up the dirt and rock hillside as I expected, but as dumb luck would have it, banks off and heads back toward the road! It gains speed…it starts to go completely straight…it's like a guided missile heading for the boulevard!

I don't swear. I hear too much of it at home and I don't like it. But as I watch the tire head down towards the main street, my thoughts are somewhere in that range right now. "&%^&*((% $##@!"

The tire, maybe going forty or fifty, who knows, makes it all the way down! It wails across the intersection but, somehow, instead of colliding broadside into a car, careens off the far-side curb and propels straight up into the air, sailing over some 10' tall cypress trees, past the sidewalk, to land innocently in a vacant yard just behind them.

Luck. Pure luck. It has come my way in both directions – bad and good. It's bad luck, but so exciting, that the tire makes it down the entire road. It's good luck that it doesn't hit somebody and mar my childhood and somebody else's life forever. Like I say, luck wears a veil. You never know how things will turn out.

Now, back to the scene on my balcony with the bird in in my gun sight. I feel a slight breeze which accompanies the warmth of this summer day. The lively green tree limbs rustle a bit as I take aim at the little target nestled in, partially hidden. I carefully press the stock of the rifle against my shoulder while supporting the barrel as best as I can with my left hand – and slowly draw my right index finger in, pressuring the trigger towards my hand. "Pow!"

"Thunk!" There's that rewarding sound again.

"Man! I've hit something!" I say to myself. I don't know if the BB has hit a limb, part of the tree trunk, or maybe even the bird!

Then, a few moments later, I hear a different sound. "Plop!" It's a noise which tells me something has hit the ground – and I'm hoping it's not a tree limb I've shot off. I'm hoping I have hit my target, and I don't mean an old, tattered paper one.

In the excitement I just drop the gun on the deck and scramble downstairs, out the front door and around the house to that side of our yard. Out of breath from running and maybe the thrill of it all, I reach the spot just under the tree. There it is, lying in the grass amidst the pine needles! Wow! I did it! I shot that bird with my (okay, Mike's) BB gun! There's no movement and a little blood showing in the feathers just below the neck. It's "dead as a doornail," as they say.

Talk about being proud: I'm ecstatic! What a shot! Who would have ever thought I could have nailed a bird that was pretty well hidden in a tree from that distance? I'm grinning. "Yes!" I exclaim out loud. "Yes!"

I remember the other time when that bird flew overhead at the park and I aimed at it in the sky, shot – and missed. As I relive that frustrating moment, I reenact the whole scene, leaning way back under the tree and looking upward as if to shoot again, actually pretending to hold the bow and arrow. "That bird didn't get away from me this time!"

A lot of the limbs are bare near the trunk of the tree, clear of pine needles. I can see a long distance up. Funny. There's a limb up there with a wad of brown pine needles sitting on it. "Why would those pine needles clump together like that half- way up the tree?" I wonder. Then I answer myself, out loud, "Because that's the bird's nest."

I realize the bird was not just resting on a limb; she was in her nest. Maybe she was warming eggs soon due to hatch. Maybe the young were already born, and she was caring for them. I have no way to know. What I do know is that I just killed a creature that meant no harm to me and was just trying to help its young survive. As I think about it, I know those little creatures will all suffer as well, either by never being born or by starving to death, waiting for food from the mother ... food which will never arrive. And this is all due to my "lucky" shot.

I dig a little hole and bury the little bird and mark a small cross in the dirt on top. I cry a bit as I meander my way back to the balcony to retrieve Mike's BB gun. Soon it's back in Mike's hands. I don't mention to him, or anyone, what I've done. I'm so ashamed. I never ask to play with his gun again. I never go out to hunt, to kill like that, again.

That little bird and its babies taught me a lesson about the preciousness of life. To this day, if I find even a spider in my home, I "catch" it with a glass and take it outside.

My "lucky" shot turns into bad luck for a bird, its family and me. The "luck," which at one moment provides me with the feeling of total success, unveils itself to deliver a sickening understanding of what I have just done.

My thrill to kill has left me. One could say I've outgrown it on this very day. One could also say that for me to achieve this realization is lucky, too. Luck keeps changing beneath its disguise.

Later on, as an adult, as I think back on my childhood, I see how fortune has smiled upon me. Had that arrow shot into the air in the park landed about a foot the other way, it would have changed two lives - for the worse. That tire crossing the boulevard without colliding into a car could have changed the lives of any number of people, including mine – for the worse. When it comes to close calls, I understand how "lucky" I truly am. I'll bet you can think of times in your life when luck smiled upon you from behind its veil. You never know.

Ah, but luck doesn't stay good or bad forever. That "lucky" shot at the dog behind the back door is one example. How am I to appreciate at age thirteen that when one keeps opening and closing a glass door, it shakes, and the tiny hole in the glass slowly begins to crack and get larger? There's now a giant split spreading up the door from the bottom corner of the glass halfway to the handle. It's rather remarkable, really. It's kind of a pretty design. You can't help noticing it now. Dad says I gotta pay for this with my allowance and by painting part of the house outside – but I'm lucky. He lets me slide on the hole in the screen.

Second Thoughts

※

Luck can come disguised, certainly. But whether it's good luck or bad, if we can learn from the experience, then we have certainly won something! Life is to be treasured. We can't create it, but sometimes we have the ability to either allow a life to go on or to end it, as when dealing with insects or animals. To mature to the point of understanding that we possess that capability, along with the responsibilities which come with it -- something the other creatures of this Earth cannot comprehend -- is the challenge we all accept by calling ourselves "Human Beings."

Dropping In Deeper

1. What does the author receive for his thirteenth birthday? Can you see yourself receiving a birthday gift like this today? Why or why not?

2. Boys and girls may go through a phase of being fascinated with killing things, and then grow out of it. What is one explanation?

3. This question is for girls to answer. Have you gone through the same phase of wanting to kill little creatures? If so, give an example. If not, what is a phase you remember going through when you were six or seven?

4. What is a lesson the story teaches about launching an arrow or firing a bullet into the air?

5. Sketch the glass back door after the author shoots it with the BB gun as your mind's eye sees it OR the old tire as it is pushed down the hill. Describe your picture with a caption.

6. What good comes from the author having killed the bird?

7. What does the author mean when he says, "Luck wears a veil?"

8. Do you think the author would have taken the shot if he had known the bird was sitting on a nest? Why or why not?

9. What lesson does the author not seem to understand immediately after both shooting the arrow at the bird and rolling the tire down the dirt street?

10. Describe a time in your life when you have been lucky with a close call.

11. Name two examples in the story of acting "on impulse."What does that mean? What is the problem with this kind of behavior?

Chapter 16: Billy Bully, Dickie Evil, And The Crazed Malibu Surfer

– *Coping With Bullies*

Most of us know the trauma of dealing with a bully, either from personal experience or by witnessing someone else's suffering. A bully can be a kid in your neighborhood or school, someone using the Internet to deliver threats and insults, or even a respected adult figure such as a neighbor, teacher, or cop.

Even after many years, the sting of an encounter with a bully can continue to brew inside of us. We keep replaying the scene and the outcome, and we harbor the wish that somehow we could have kept it from happening. It still upsets us to recall the incident. The event can be physical, as in being hit or assaulted, or emotional, as in being badgered and teased. It's important to understand that "things happen" and to realize that bullies prey upon our weaknesses. We need someone to turn to for guidance. That person can help us avoid or handle a bully or lead us to discover a way to cope with the physical and emotional damage. Let me see if I can help through the telling of these stories.

I'm six years old. My family has just moved to this really nice neighborhood in the Philadelphia suburbs, and it's a hot and humid morning in late summer. School hasn't started up yet. I'm out to make friends.

Bryn Mawr Elementary School calls to me. It's a classic three-story brick schoolhouse, not including the underground basement level, surrounded on two sides by a huge grass field with only a four-foot-high hedge separating it from adjacent streets. It's like a school you might see in a Hollywood film from the 1950s. The asphalt playground area close to the building boasts giant fifteen-foot-tall swings, a carousel with eight steel handles so you can hold on as the speed increases, an eight-foot-high shiny steel slide, a pole with six rings hanging down on chains connected to a ball-bearing hub so you can run and grip tightly with both hands as your feet fly upward and outward, and a seesaw large enough for two kids to sit on each end.

One side of the building boasts a three-story red brick wall with no windows. Kids love to throw tennis balls as high as they can without losing them on the roof. I am to lose many tennis balls there. Best of all, the school is only one block away from my house down my tree-lined residential street.

I know Philadelphia is going to be a lot different from my former home in Georgia. For example, people here have a different way of speaking. Instead of calling to someone by saying, "Y'all," people like to shout, "Hey yo!" Another lesser-known fact is that people here, mostly the guys, like to communicate using "sign language." I am to discover that each finger of the hand, when held up, sometimes combined with one or two others, has a special meaning. Every one of those meanings is an insult. This is not to be confused with the Italian hand gestures or the wimpy "One finger says it all." It's a lot more than that. Whatever the selection of fingers, you've been sworn at. So, instead of yelling, a guy can simply put up some fingers and the profanity-filled words stand delivered. It's a very effective technique, especially when utilized in heavy traffic by drivers with rolled up car windows. I don't recall seeing any girls communicating this way, but they probably do. Welcome to my new neighborhood.

It's a hot day and I'm curious to see if anybody is on the playground. I dash down the block and reach the corner across from my soon-to-be school's hedges and bushes lining its perimeter. Looking down I see there's a contractor's punch in the concrete that displays the year 1946. I will soon learn not to stand on it when I'm around other kids – lest I get punched myself!

It's great being so small. I can squeeze through openings in the hedge and make it to the grass field without a scratch, avoiding having to walk on the sidewalk all the way around to the entrance. I look across the yard and there are two kids on the seesaw. Yes! They're about 100 yards distant. I'm only beginning my way toward them when they spot me. I happily wave and smile because I'm glad to discover new friends on my first venture out! Neither one of them waves back, but they both climb off the seesaw and head my way to greet me.

As they get closer, I give them a cheery, "Hi!" I only remember a few disconnected moments after that.

For instance, I can see the sunlight glinting off the shiny belt buckle of one of the kids as I look up at him from the ground. How I arrived there I don't know! He's fully occupied with jumping up and down on my stomach. Apparently, he's bored with the playground equipment and has found me to be the perfect new apparatus to enjoy! I'm crying out …no, I'm just crying. There's no one else anywhere close by who can help me.

I recall the guys taking turns stomping on me and eventually getting tired, or bored, so off they go, running away, leaving me covered in cuts and scrapes which read, "Welcome to the Neighborhood!" I pick up my crumpled little self and stagger back home, this time choosing to use the asphalt path that meets the sidewalk. It's a longer route home, but I'm not in good enough shape to manage crawling through the hedge at the moment.

Mom's home. She's upset that I'm hurt but manages to patch up my cuts with Band-Aids and some TLC. She tells me to recount what happened. I do. Amazingly, within a week she has somehow contacted the school principal, discovered that the kid with the shiny belt buckle is the notorious Billy, has spoken with his mom, AND has arranged for a lunch on an upcoming Saturday at his house in order for Billy to apologize for beating me up. Wow!

Noontime that Saturday arrives, and Mom and I stand at Billy's front door. His house is a lot smaller and simpler than ours. His mother answers our knock, invites us in, and the three of us sit down at a small table where a turkey sandwich lunch awaits us. It turns out that nine-year-old Billy doesn't have a dad and he's an only child. He likes his hair curly, so he uses his mother's beauty salon hair dryer to give him the curls. He smokes cigarettes. Oh, and he has chosen to skip lunch with us, so he's out playing somewhere.

The sandwich is fine.

I should add, he never does hassle me again. Thanks, Mom, for not over-reacting to the incident and for finding a way to make the problem go away.

Summers tend to bring challenges my way. When I'm seven, just as summer starts, I come down with measles to be followed by chicken pox, which then leads to the mumps, one right after the other! There are no vaccines at this time for "childhood diseases" like that. I lose a chunk of my summer to these darn illnesses! In these days, if you're a kid and get the mumps, you must stay in a dark room for at least a week because doctors believe your vision might be affected by bright light.

Another first day of summer the following year starts off with my brother pulling the blanket out from under me. I happen to be standing on top of our bunk bed at the time. I fall, hitting my head on the floor, and end up with a mild concussion. It means a week of not getting to play outside.

Still later that same summer, I need Mom's help with handling a bully of another kind.

Summers in Philadelphia tend to be hot and unbearably humid. It is said that when it was the nation's capital, Congress would shut down for part of the summer because of all the bickering and yelling attributed to the miserable weather. My family finds the New Jersey shoreline just south of Atlantic City to be the perfect summer escape. Dad stays in town in Philadelphia to work and comes to us in Longport for the weekends.

Each summer we stay in my great-grandmother's huge three-story Victorian beach house, built atop an above-ground basement. Right in front of the house runs a small boardwalk adjacent to a concrete seawall. The sounds of this house are a mixture of the white noise of breaking ocean waves, squawking seagulls, sea breezes whistling through the crusty metal screens of open windows, and the ringing of the nearby church bells every hour.

It's dark and creepy down in the basement with its one car garage piled up with junk, a maid's room and bathroom, and a gray slate-wall shower with concrete flooring which is so great for warming up after a couple of hours of beach time. The sunlight reaches it from ventilation screens on top. I lean in, facing the corner of the shower, my little hands grasped behind me, and let the water just splatter down my back. Ecstasy! It's easy to just daydream as I stand there, that is, until the hot water runs out. There's a splintery staircase leading up to the kitchen from the darkness, but more interestingly, there are dingy spaces and unlit sections all around under the house – places I've never explored for fear of black widows and wandering rats and whatever else roams there at night.

The ocean temperature is in the 70s, the waves are fun, and the sand is white and warm and welcoming, especially to lie upon after coming in chilled from riding the waves on my blow-up canvas raft. Sometimes the mosquito truck comes by gushing out its white fog insecticide. I don't know that it's a mosquito truck or what insecticide is. It's so much fun to run behind. I do that with my little brother until one day the driver stops, leans out, and yells, "Your hair will turn green if you run in the stuff!" That's the end of truck chasing for me! I don't want green hair! Longport is a wonderful place to be a kid, except, there just aren't that many kids in our neighborhood.

It is here, at the innocent age of seven, that I meet Dickie. He might be ten years old. He has an older brother, George, who's maybe fourteen. George is kind of quiet, owns a beautiful 3-speed English racer bike, and smokes cigarettes. Dickie always seems to be up for some kind of mischief, but most of this goes on when I'm not around.

His house is a bit smaller than ours but has the same aboveground basement design. His family owns the only TV we know about on the block. I admit that's probably a major reason I like to go over there. Like I say, Dickie does some peculiar things at times. For instance, one afternoon he and I are in his basement when he tells me about his remote-controlled plane. I'm curious! I've never seen one up close.

"It's over there in the closet," he tells me, pointing to an unpainted closed door.

"I want to see it!" I tell him.

Over we go as he opens the door to an almost empty closet. The basement has no working light fixtures, and the little light that exists comes from wood lattice venting which opens to the outdoors. So, the inside of the closet is mysteriously dark, but I can see something in the back corner. To me it looks like a live bait basket for fishing, but I can't really tell.

"Where is it?" I wonder out loud.

Dickie points to whatever it is and says, "That's it. Take a look."

As I lean in a bit to see it better, he attempts to push me all the way into the closet and slam the door shut! I jump back enough to keep clear of the slamming door and yell, "Why'd you do that?"

Dickie never answers, and I leave and head for home. No TV today.

Little kids can forgive and forget, and that I do.

Until another time…

Dickie and I are once again in the basement. It's just a little after I've been on the beach, so I'm barefoot wearing only my damp dark blue swim trunks with little white sailboats all over them. I can't talk him into going up to watch TV, so this is where we end up. He's saying stuff I really don't understand and then he grabs me. He tells me, "Take off your swim trunks."

"Huh?' is all I can say.

"I want you drop your swim trunks. My brother, George, made me a bet I couldn't make you do it."

I'm still thinking about going up and watching TV. He's towering over me and gives me a really serious look. So, I untie my swim trunks, they slip down to my ankles, and there I stand, naked, except for my feet covered up by the swimsuit. He drops down to his knees right in front of me. I can still see the top of his head and then, moments later, him looking up into my confused little kid's eyes. I will always remember that strange sensation. Always.

Then Dickie says, "Don't tell anybody about this."

I have no idea what this is all about and think it's pretty silly. After a couple of minutes, he just walks away, heading up the basement stairs. I pull up my dark blue swim trunks with little white sailboats all over them. I know this is not a good time to try to follow him so I can watch TV. I find the screen door to the outside and get along home, which is only three houses away.

Of course, I tell Mom what has happened.

She doesn't say much. So, I go barefoot back to the seawall, watch the waves a minute, and decide to go swimming, right in front of the lifeguard tower as Mom requires.

The funny thing is, though, Dickie never comes by to play or invites me over to watch TV anymore. He and his brother George just fade away from my life. I do find another boy, closer to my age, to play with. He's from New York and lives with his grandpa. We go fishing together.

Years later, as I look back upon this incident with Dickie, I'm grateful to Mom for not showing that she was upset, for not traumatizing me with a shriek or all sorts of emotion when I told her about what happened. Once again, she "called the principal." I know she had words with Dickie's mom. I also know I never was made to feel truly disturbed by it all. "Uncomfortable and confused" would be proper descriptors. I just didn't understand the significance of the incident at that time. I can live with that. Thanks Mom.

A few decades later, as an adult, I am to meet another bully, this time while surfing Malibu. I bring this upon myself. I fail to anticipate how badly things can go. Mom can't help me this time.

It's late afternoon in summer and there's about a four-foot swell breaking. The waves here at Malibu have beautiful form because while the beach is sandy, the waves actually come in over the submerged rocks at three points. This means that there isn't much sand shifting around on the ocean bottom affecting the way a wave breaks – they're consistent. A point means there's a buildup of underwater rocks jutting out into the ocean, so the wave doesn't just collapse all at once, but "peels" off in one direction. A surfer can ride in blue water, just ahead of the breaking white water of the wave. The ride often turns into a long one… if no one gets in the way.

As the sun comes close to setting, I paddle into one of the First Point waves at Malibu, but a guy takes off in front of me! That's not proper surf etiquette. The person first on the wave, closest to the break, normally has the right of way. In a perfect World, this means that the surfer gets to ride it alone. However, often another surfer will break this rule and drop in on the other's wave.

This is happening to me, and I'm not pleased. I intend to get a nose ride on the wave, meaning I work my way up to the nose area of the board as it continues across the wave. My goal is to get at least five toes over the nose of the board as I ride; it really looks cool from the beach and is a fun challenge. But that's almost impossible now with someone riding in front of me on the same wave. In my high school days, I didn't just take it. There were times I would leap off my surfboard and tackle the surfer riding so rudely in front of me! We'd fall in the water together and if he wanted more, we'd sometimes tussle, have a fistfight, even end up on the beach to finish it. I never even suffered a bloody lip on these occasions. Of course, that was back in high school.

As I've matured over the years, so has my technique for handling situations like this. Now I perform my special "jerk the jerk" maneuver, which I've resorted to numerous times at different beaches. This is in the days before surf leashes, so falling off a surfboard usually means a swim back to the shoreline in order to retrieve it.

I guide my longboard right below and behind his, lean over, and grasp the back end (tail block) of his board, and jerk it back and forth one time. As a result, he loses his footing and ends up falling off. I then skillfully turn my board down, away from him and his out-of-control surfboard, and ride on. On occasion, if his loose board is still rolling along in the wave, I've even masterfully picked it up as I'm riding and carried it to the beach, righteously dumping it on the sand before paddling back out. It's kind of a nice "finishing touch." On this occasion, I manage to "jerk the jerk" perfectly and get that rather nice nose ride. The guy's board washes in with the wave behind me all the way to the sand.

As I paddle back to the lineup, quite pleased with myself, I look over and notice the fellow halfway to the beach, swimming in to retrieve his surfboard. He turns around and spots me, and even from thirty yards away, with twilight approaching, I can make out his angry stare.

Normally, I would just ignore a guy like that and paddle out for another wave. But I figure I'm going to probably have to deal with him out in the lineup anyway, and I'm still upset that he cut me off on the wave. I paddle toward him to show who's boss. I feel I had every right to remove him from the wave the way I did.

Instead of turning away and heading for his board which is washed up on the sand, what I expect him to do, he swims toward me! We meet within moments. He's right by the nose of my surfboard now, glaring up at me as I sit on my board like a perched pheasant. These two large gnarly hands come up out of the water, grasp both sides of the nose of my board, and in another moment, he's sitting on it with me! I must shift back a bit past the middle of the board to accommodate him and to maintain balance. It must be quite a sight, two grown men sitting on one longboard as they face each other. I realize that his hands are not the only gnarly aspect to him. I hadn't noticed until now how large a guy he is! He looks like a wrestler and his face appears to have taken the brunt of some major confrontations.

"Hit me!" he screams. "Go on! Ahole!"

"I'm not going to do that!" is my not-so-sly reply, understanding that this huge guy is just waiting for me make physical contact with him so he can unload on me.

"I want you to hit me. You're a good surfer. I've seen you. You didn't have to knock me off my board like that!"

After thinking for just a moment, I come back at him again with a not-so-clever, "I'm not going to hit you."

"You chicken____ motherf_____. You ass____. Come on weenie and hit me!"

Unfortunately, there are no waves at the moment, so everyone around us in the water finds all of this quite entertaining. I'm consistent as I calmly answer him again, "I'm not going to hit you." He remains settled in sitting on the opposite end of my board.

"Then you're not going to get a single wave to yourself. I'll be right there with you on every one!"

We're at a stalemate now. Sure, the bruiser wants little ol' me to hit him once so he can pummel me. I'm not going to bite. I shake the surfboard just a bit by shifting my hips, he loses his balance on the narrow nose section and falls off! I figure I'm toast now. Maybe he's going to drown me.

But instead, the guy glances at me with an "I'm gonna get you!" look and starts swimming in for his board. Whew! Within a few minutes he's back out, though, positioning himself right beside me to be there for any wave I try to catch. I could paddle up to Second Point to try to avoid him, but it will get darker sooner there, being farther from any lights on the pier, and I really don't think he's going to let me off that easily. So, I stay.

He's true to his word. I paddle for a wave, and he paddles. I pull out immediately so he can have the wave to himself. I can only hope another will come along before he returns. This routine repeats itself several times for the next few minutes until divine intervention intercedes; it's truly a miracle!

As dusk takes hold, a surfer younger and much larger than me makes the mistake of taking off on a wave in front of the bruiser! I see them riding side by side in the dimming light, silhouetted against the car headlights streaking along the Coast Highway just beyond the beach and the bright Malibu Pier as its light pierces the now dark ocean water. It's rather a pretty sight, worthy of a photo or a painting.

They're both gone longer than I would expect. Eventually, the new guy paddles back out to us, and he's sporting a bloody nose! "That guy's crazy! He wanted to fight me over that wave!"

Suspicions confirmed. Any doubts that maybe I misunderstood the situation now evaporate. It's time for me to go in. It's getting really dark.

As I look toward the beach in the dimness, there's the guy! He's standing on the shore looking out toward us -- toward me if he could see me! Fortunately, I'm camouflaged as I'm in the mix of other surfers, all of us in black wetsuits. I figure he wants to use the cover of darkness to settle matters with me. I'm anxious to not provide him with the opportunity.

I decide to paddle up the coast in the fading light to Second Point. I paddle into shore without catching a wave. Then I hustle along by the rear of the beach along the fence behind the restrooms like a scampering rat, jet up the staircase, throw my board on top of my car, fasten only one strap, jump in soaking wet, and careen out of there!

For the next several months, I'm always on the lookout for that guy, no matter which beach I'm surfing. He becomes my secret terror. It's evident to me he's a good candidate for making the evening news regarding a road rage incident. I'm certain he's like that elephant who never forgets a person who mistreated him and years later crushes him to death. Whenever I paddle out, I'm scouring the other surfers in case he's there; I want to spot him first! During these months, surfing becomes a mixture of joy and dread. Eventually, the bruiser fades away from my daily thoughts, but it takes a long time. I don't know what I would do if I were to see him again – except run.

I have since retired my patented "jerk the jerk" maneuver. Oh, I'll yell at a guy sometimes for dropping in on my wave, but that's as far as it goes. You never can tell about someone. You never quite know.

Second Thoughts

※

Facing a bully at some point seems inevitable. Most of us will not only suffer a bully's mean and possibly violent exploits, but at times we might find ourselves acting like a bully ourselves! It may be in the role of being the older brother or sister, or something said sometime to someone younger and smaller when we're trying to impress our friends. It's part of living life. What matters is how we choose to react to a bully's actions, how we manage to cope, and how quickly we recognize when we are slipping into that role of being a bully and manage to change our direction.

Dropping In Deeper

1. How does the author manage to lose tennis balls?

2. At the time of the story, what is the purpose of the "sign language" people use in Philadelphia?

3. What does the author do which helps him cope with bullies in his life?

4. The incident with Dickie could be very upsetting to anyone. What does the author's mother do which helps him not be as traumatized as he could be?

5. Do you think the bruiser is a bully? Why or why not?

6. Sketch a picture of the bruiser and the other surfer riding the wave in together as your mind's eye sees it, OR the playground where the author "meets" Billy.

7. Have you had to face a bully? What happened? If not, what story about a bully do you know? Briefly explain it.

8. If you encounter a bully on the Internet or at school, what can you do about it to avoid having the incident brew inside of you for years?

9. How much do you blame the author for the Malibu incident? Why?

10. Can you think of a time you have acted like a bully yourself? Briefly describe how it happened.

Chapter 17: The Gift

- Thinking Before You Act &
You Can't Please Everyone

Paula Bickford

Girls seem to socialize, interact, and gather together more easily than boys. I think it has to do with their gift with words. Most begin to speak at a younger age than boys, and a girl's vocabulary tends to be more advanced in the early elementary school years.

Here's an example of this difference. You might find it serves as a measure of "the gift." It's a lesson for which years of college and even a Master's Degree in Education have not prepared me.

I'm a teacher, in my late 30s, and my fifth-grade class has just come back into the classroom after the lunch break. One of the boys, Juan, is upset. He's crying! How can he be feeling so poorly right after playing his heart out at recess?

Leaving the classroom door open, I give everyone their tasks and invite Juan to my "office," the space just outside the doorway to the classroom. He stands in front of the open door, out of view of the others, and I stand in the doorway, in view of the class but out of earshot. This way I maintain control of everything.

"What happened?"

"Charlie from Room 24 pushed me hard against the handball wall," he stammers.

"Why did he do that?" I query.

"I don't know."

I send a student with a note requesting Charlie's presence.

Several minutes pass and Charlie arrives. I seat the two boys on the "witness stand," a bench I keep near the doorway where I can sit between them and still have a view of the classroom. Placing myself in the middle avoids any impulsive, angry moves by the parties involved. It helps to "cool them off." I admit a bit of favoritism kicks in as I presume Charlie, the student from the other classroom, is the culprit in this situation and I give him the business.

"Juan tells me you shoved him against the handball wall. If you have a problem with one of MY students, and you can't work it out, you come to me and let me know. I'll take care of it. I promise. Don't you dare do anything to one of MY students. If you do, you might as well push me! Now what happened out there? Juan, you just listen to Charlie's explanation. Don't say anything. You'll have your chance in a minute."

His eyes tell me that 10-year-old Charlie takes me seriously. "Well, Juan bumped me while we were playing handball and I fell down. He and a bunch of the guys laughed when it happened. I got mad."

Juan starts up, "Well, he…"

"Juan, you'll have your chance in a minute. Let him talk."

"So, Charlie, then you pushed him against the wall. Do you think Juan bumped you on purpose?"

"I don't know. I don't think so. But I don't like people laughing at me."

Juan then has his chance to explain. Along the way Charlie tries to butt in and I stop him. "You had your time. Now let Juan take his turn." There are a few discrepancies, but mostly loose facts between them that I masterfully manage to tie together into a nice, neat bow. I'm really proud of myself for being so good at this. It's clear it's basically a misunderstanding. Charlie overreacted, for sure, and could be sent to the principal's office. But Juan has some blame to share as well.

"All right, you two. We can't have this sort of thing happening on the playground or after school. You both share some blame in this. If I hear of this happening again, it will go straight to the principal. Now, I don't expect you to shake hands or be best friends or anything like that. But can you "peacefully coexist" out there and not hassle each other? That means after school and on the way home, as well. Now I mean it, one word of a problem and it's straight to the principal. There better be no more trouble between you two."

They agree. They shake hands anyway. Charlie trots back to his class and I resume being a teacher with a text-oriented social studies lesson to present to the whole class.

This has been rather a "real life" social studies lesson for the pair. Overall, I find that in dealing with boys, if we get the matter out in the open and discuss it, we can usually come to some sort of resolution.

I never ever hear of another problem between the two after that incident. End of story. I go home that afternoon feeling really good about being an involved teacher who helps his students work out their issues.

Quick side note: This technique of telling a student from another class that if he pushes one of MY students he might as well be pushing me, has served its purpose over the years. One time, a few years earlier, while teaching 7th grade at a middle school, there was a similar after-lunch situation. After noticing that one of my students was quite upset, he revealed that an 8th grader had been extorting him for his lunch money by bullying him on a daily basis.

I spoke to another teacher about it and the next day at mid-morning break we set out on the yard after this fellow. After we called out his name and approached him, he ran from us. He knew he was in trouble. We followed him all over the playground until the two of us had him cornered against a fence. With a very serious expression on my face, I gave him the same "as you do unto one of my students, you do unto me" statement, telling him to stop stealing lunch money, and I warned him not to go after that student outside of school, either. I kept track of things after that incident. He gave up his life of crime on the spot, at least when it came to being a bully and taking kids' lunch money.

Today a teacher could be in serious trouble for taking action like this. But in those days, it was an approach that appeared effective.

Now, back to 5th grade a few years down the line. It's another day. The students have returned after lunch recess and there's 9-year-old Jeanie in tears. I see she's really upset, so I invite her to my "office" just as before with Juan and Charlie.

"What's wrong?" I inquire.

I'm going to leave out some of what she recounts. Otherwise, it would require another page. As I said, girls have a way with words! Apparently, there's some kind of name-calling issue with another girl in a different classroom.

I send for the student, Terri, and we go through the same procedure.

They sit on "the witness stand" with me in the middle to prevent any provocation, any kind of hassle between them, as Jeanie tearfully describes what happened. "Terri hit a double-bounce at handball and I…"

Terri cuts in, "But she opened her hand…"

I stop them both and remind them that each one gets to explain what happened, uninterrupted by the other.

Jeanie continues, "So, I told her that wasn't fair, and she lost, and she got mad and hit the ball really hard against the wall so I'd have to go chase it. Then she said I was stupid."

"Okay," I say. "Jeanie, you had your chance to explain. Now Terri, what's your side to this?"

Terri begins, "At the lunch table Jeanie said I was eating a stinky sandwich."

Jeanie cuts in, "No I didn't. I ...."

I stop Jeanie, reminding her that this is Terri's turn, and ask Terri to continue. She does. I'm not making much sense of it all but then I ask Jeanie, "Did you?"

"No! I just told Sonia we need to hurry and grab a handball court."

"Well, Terri, what about the double-bounce hit?" I inquire.

"That didn't happen. After I hit the ball Jeanie fell and couldn't get to it. Then she said I hit a slicie and it wasn't fair." (A slicie, for those new to the game, is a shot where the handball just skims the ground and hits the very bottom of the backboard. Such a shot tends to just dribble onto the ground making it impossible to hit - thus it's illegal.)

I'm getting nowhere with them. I need to get back to teaching in the classroom, anyway. I can't seem to find that little nugget of truth they both share in common in their stories so I can neatly tie things together in a lovely bow in order to solve the matter. So, I cut it short with the speech about "peaceful coexistence" and that there will be real trouble if they bother each other anymore. They understand and return to their classrooms. Nobody shakes hands.

Ah, another crisis settled. I don't exactly feel the same satisfaction as with Juan and Charlie, but I know I'm doing the right thing by being involved and expressing my interest in the two students. I'm still feeling okay about things as I return home at the end of the day.

As to the crisis being settled... a few weeks later I ask Jeanie how things are going. I'm just checking up on matters to demonstrate

I really do care about everyone. I know she appreciates my concern.

"Well, they're okay. Only Terri told Sonia and Shanice not to speak to me anymore. So, they don't."

Indeed, the complexities of language and relationships, that the girls saw a way not to directly defy what I said, but instead talked to their friends and had them get involved, often come into play at an earlier age for girls than boys. I would see scenarios like this repeated over my many years of teaching.

While boys at age ten may tend to deal simply in whether something is right or wrong, girls of that age often explore the gray area between what we say and what we do and how we explain it. In would seem girls often experience the gift of exploration and expressing themselves at this time in their lives sooner than boys who tend to mature a bit later.

Second Thoughts

※

My mom used to tell me, "The road to hell is paved with good intentions." Many times in our lives we set out to do the right thing, thinking it is for the benefit of everyone, only to find out later that not everyone looks at things the same way. Some are unhappy with what you have done. You just can't please everyone all the time. I certainly found this as a teacher, with both students and parents. Sometimes, it may not be a matter of your intentions or goal being at fault, but just the way you go about it that makes the difference to others.

Think before you act whenever possible. Weigh the consequences of your actions as best you can. Your worst enemy can be impulsiveness, reacting immediately to a problem by starting out to deal with it without figuring out a strategy. When someone asks a question or makes a remark, there is no stopwatch going which requires you to blurt out a response. Take your time. Think about what you're going to say before you utter the words. Once you say them, your words can be a supporting witness to what you have done or can be held against you forever. In these days of social media and instant communication, this lesson is particularly appropriate. What we say and do should be the gift we give to others.

Dropping In Deeper

1. "His eyes tell me that 10-year-old Charlie takes me seriously." What does this mean?

2. When you do something, what can be your worst enemy? Why?

3. Sketch the author in his "office" speaking to Juan as your mind's eye sees it OR the scene on the playground as Jeanie describes it. Describe your picture with a caption.

4. Give the definition of "impulsive" as in "...avoids any impulsive, angry moves..." Use it in a sentence.

5. Why do you think the boys shake hands after the meeting even though the teacher tells them that it's not necessary?

6. How was the 8th grade bully using "extortion" against one of the author's students?

7. Describe a time you have done something impulsively. What was the result?

8. What would you do if a bully at school started demanding your lunch money (or something else)?

9.Describe a time you had a problem on the playground. How did it end?

10. Did you believe at first that the whole thing was settled between Jeanie and Terri? Why or why not?

11. Tell what you think "the gift" is. There is more than just one possible answer to this question. Provide one. You don't have to explain your answer.

Chapter 18: Close Call

– *Recognizing When To Quit & Changing Goals*

Do you have a favorite waterfall you've seen or managed to swim under? Maybe you've managed to sit behind some falls where you can watch the water pouring down in front of you, looking and sounding like a force field ray from Star Wars or Star Trek. From that experience, even if you've never been in the ocean, you can begin to appreciate the thrill and awesomeness of swimming in and riding on ocean waves.

Waves break or collapse differently all over the World. Some crumble over as the crest gives way to gravity and the water tumbles the same way an avalanche or rockslide rumbles down a mountain. The size of the wave helps determine just how forceful this flow of water can be. In other places, the crest pitches, throwing itself out in front of the wave, crashing powerfully onto the surface as it creates a momentary "tube." Surfers often strive to surf inside that tube, riding parallel to the beach, with the wave momentarily surrounding them. Surfers don't just go straight toward shore when taking off on a wave. Otherwise, they would just get walloped as tons of seawater cascade down upon them. When riding a wave that has form to it, the surfer can stay ahead of the crashing water. Otherwise, going straight toward the beach could be like trying to stand under a massive waterfall.

There are waves that wobble like a giant bowl of Jello. There are others that look like a crane has scooped out chunks of them, appearing more like the side of a dented automobile than waves. Others swirl as if they're inside a witch's cauldron. Part of the mystique of ocean wave lies in their many forms, shapes and moods.

The ocean bottom affects the way waves break. In Hawaii, waves differ from their California relatives in part because Hawaii has coral reefs that interact with the moving water differently than California's rocks and sand. Also, California has a continental shelf, a raised ocean bottom extending anywhere from one-half to several miles out to sea, which then drops off into deep ocean. When the waves or ground swells approach the shoreline in California, they lose some of their energy and speed because of the drag created by traveling over the continental shelf.

In Hawaii, where there is no continental shelf, these same swells slam into the islands – which you may know are actually underwater mountain tops -- at full speed. The waves travel faster as they approach the beaches and carry much more force than the California ones. Surfers visiting the Hawaiian Islands suddenly realize this difference when the fast-moving white water of a Hawaiian wave that has just broken in front of them first pounds them. It takes a while to adjust to that greater power.

For those on the East Coast, there is an even larger continental shelf that makes for smaller waves than in Hawaii or California. But on occasion, a hurricane or Nor'easter in the Atlantic Ocean can generate swells to match the height and power of many California surf spots.

Now that you and I share a basic understanding of ocean waves, I begin my tale. I want you to see everything through my eyes so you can better understand how I manage to get myself into such a bind.

It's mid-December, a gorgeous Hawaiian winter morning with blue sky and a few patches of gentle white clouds. The air temperature hovers in the high 70s, the same as the ocean water - there's hardly any breeze. I'm in my mid sixties and I've been vacationing in Princeville on the north side of the island of Kauai with my wife for the past week, but must return to California later that same day. It's my last chance to surf and a new swell has arrived overnight. By that I mean the waves have jumped in size and this could last maybe a few hours or up to a few days. The second high surf warning of the week is occurring. I want to surf it.

I have a 9'6" rented California-style longboard under my arm. It's designed for the slower California waves, certainly not for large Hawaiian surf. It's fine for beginners to use on small waves in Hawaii; that's why it's available. I know the make of the board and have surfed on this model in California many times, so I'm comfortable with it for some fair-sized surf.

I survey the surf from a bluff, home of the Princeville Resort Kauai. It's on the east side of Hanalei Bay, close to the bay's opening, tucked in and protected from the large swells generated by winter storms in Alaska's Aleutian Islands region. During heavy swells, these massive waves march into Hanalei Bay after their 2,200-mile journey, pouring their energy upon the reefs toward the middle and west side. Kauai, as the northern most island in Hawaii, is the first stop for these northwest swells sent by way of Alaska.

The waves, which break about a quarter of a mile out from the resort, can be deceiving. Their height and power are difficult to evaluate because they're distant and I'm looking down at them from the hotel's sundeck. It appears it might be a tad larger than it was a few days ago when I surfed last. I recall how startled I was by the grinding sound just behind me as I streaked across one of the waves that day. It wasn't a sound I'm accustomed to in California, and it told me there's a lot of energy in these waves. The crest was about six feet above my head – not big by Hawaiian standards - but it packed a lot of punch. I don't need anything any bigger.

Paddling out from the hotel's private beach is fairly easy today. There's shallow water and a reef to negotiate, but it's clear all the way to the bottom and, as I said, the swells don't tend to hit this side of the bay. Heck, as I enter the water to begin my quarter-mile paddle to the west, kids and their families surround me as they wade in the tiny waves. There's no lifeguard nearby, the closest being another quarter mile south on the sandy public beach at the end of the bay – too far away from the surfers to be of much assistance.

As I paddle and get closer to the first breakers, the roar of the ocean and how the surfers riding them look smaller against the wave than I had expected impress me. There's a lot of intensity in the swells, apparently more than a few days ago. I can't be certain. Someone skiing a new mountain or playing a new golf course must do so numerous times to become more familiar in order to improve their game. Likewise, I haven't surfed here often enough to really "know" the break and how to judge its varying conditions.

I'm not a kid anymore. I've been a surfer now over 50 years. I have ridden waves around the World, including in Japan, Australia, England, Hawaii, Mexico, the East Coast, and all over California. I'm no novice. Many say I have the "look" of a surfer, and I am proud to be one. Because of that, I'm yearning to catch at least one good wave to make my day and my surf trip a total success- and to maintain my personal surf prowess.

The ocean surface looks deceptively calm. Everything from the sun to the wind to the waves is perfect! It's like I'm in a "Come visit Hawaii" commercial. I approach the take-off area where about twenty surfers wait for "their" wave. My hair is still dry from an uneventful paddle out. I scan the horizon and see some bumps approaching about 200 yards away, right where a moment before there was just flat ocean. I'm not waiting to see what the others around me do; I churn for that horizon like a running back streaks for the goal line. It turns out to be a really good idea!

Apparently, the wave I spot is exceptionally large for the morning because no one is out that far waiting to catch it. That would indicate that the swell might be building, with more to come. It's a perfect wave, too. It's beyond anything I ever drew on the cover of my binder way back in algebra class. I'm witnessing, no, I'm actually living the part of Murph the Surf, a surf cartoon character drawn by Surfer Magazine's Rick Griffin. Murph is always in great surf and amazing situations. This one is now mine.

I paddle up the face, all ten to twelve feet of it, and I know that if this was twenty years ago, I might have swung around on my short board and gone for it. But, like Peter Pan's Wendy, I have lost the ability to "fly" like I used to. I'm older and I must accept that I don't know the waves here very well. Riding such a wave now is beyond me. Bummer!

I manage to get over its peak and it breaks just behind me, dousing me with its wind-driven spray, snapping me out of my reverie about how magical it all looks. Yes, there is only a breeze this day, but the wave creates its own wind as it rises, scooping up air while driving toward shore. Maybe you've seen pictures or paintings of seagulls, gliding along the face of a wave, lifted by the gentle wind generated by the moving water. But wait, I'm jolted by the sight of another feathering peak, the white water forming at the top and about to dump down. It's just beyond this one! I scramble and just make it up and over. Whew!

As I sit on my board between sets, I take a second to look around me. Except for a group of guys on fairly short stand-up boards, everyone else has a shortboard. No other longboarders are surfing this day. My surf watch tells me it's around 8:30. I really should be out of the water by 9:30 so I can return to the hotel in time to pack for the trip home.

During this period of calm, one of the stand-up surfers works his way over to me. As I sit on my board, I must look up into the sun as he towers over me. There's no way to make out his face, but he has a full head of blonde hair and wears only trunks and a surf vest. There's no missing his dynamic physique. He's the epitome of the surfer image. He asks, "What time is it?"

I look at my watch, even though I already know the answer. "It's eight-thirty."

"Good!"

"No, not so good," is my response as he moves out of direct line with the sun. "I have to leave around nine-thirty." I can see his face now against the brilliant blue sky. It's World-renowned surfer Laird Hamilton. This guy has ridden some of the most massive waves ever. Hanalei Bay is one of his homes. Like I said, he likes the surf when it's big. He soon returns to his place in the lineup. Everyone gives Laird any wave he wants. No hassles!

It remains a beautiful sunlit day. My intentions are to catch a couple of waves, whatever comes my way, but I am ever wary of getting mangled by one of the huge ones. As time goes by, I just can't quite manage to drop into one of these beauties, either because someone else has already caught it or my timing stinks as I try to paddle into the wave but am unable to get into it. It feels like I'm jinxed. I was able to ride three days ago! I'm just not meant to get the wave I want. I mean, as I paddle to catch one and peer over the edge of it, I see that perfectly scooped out, tapering face beckoning to me. But I can't quite drop in.

This goes on for another hour and a half. Yup, I'm way over my time limit, but still seeking that elusive wave. And in a deja vu-moment, up comes Laird Hamilton again. "What time is it?" he inquires.

I confess to him, "Ten o'clock."

"I thought you said you had to leave by nine-thirty!"

"Yup," is all I can manage, kind of looking down at the water. He leaves me again to rejoin his posse in the lineup. Every surfer knows how difficult it can be to get that "One Last Wave" before heading back to the beach. At times, there's a lull and for no reason the waves just stop. But I confess, other times that last wave you do catch is so good that instead of heading in, you turn around looking for "just one more." I'm telling you, that quest for the "One Last Wave" has even cost some of us a relationship!

Those who don't surf can still understand a surfer's obsession and that "One Last Wave" temptation. If you're a golfer, musician, computer gamer, artist, car enthusiast, or just crazy about any hobby...well, then you know what I'm talking about. Just one last game or maybe ten minutes more before we must call it a day is all we ask. Sometimes it's too much for those waiting for us.

I gradually let myself drift over a bit closer to the hotel beach. One more paddle for a smaller wave, but again, I even miss this one! Maybe I'm tired. I don't know. But I do know I'm done. I'm so done. No waves. Defeated. Downtrodden. Discouraged. I keep my head down as I exit the surf and trudge up the beach past everyone. I don't qualify as a surfer today.

I shake my head and then look up at that blue sky above. I guess it just wasn't meant to be.

I meet one guy on the path to my car. He asks me how it was, and I let him know the conditions are great but a bit challenging. He mentions that the swell today is much larger than the one earlier in the week.

"How so?" I ask. "I was here Monday. The waves don't look that much bigger."

"Yeah," he responds, "but here the waves tend to get thicker rather than taller. They're breaking much harder than on Monday. It's pretty dangerous."

I think of Laird Hamilton and his buddies and the fact that they're out there surfing on this particular day. I didn't see him on Monday. I'm starting to understand.

A few moments later, I'm back at my car and it hits me. No, not the car. No, not the board. I realize I was the only longboarder out there for a reason.

I finally connect the dots as I recall a huge day in California…

A few years earlier on a gray winter's morning, I'm at a surf break called "Swami's" in Encinitas, California. Its name comes from the golden-domed Sikh-style architecture of the Self Realization Center on the cliff above it. The surf that day remains some of the largest waves I've ever seen in person in Southern California – pushing twenty-foot faces. Honest. I'm content just to watch waves this day, I don't have to ride them. I know they are beyond my capabilities.

Occasionally, an outside set comes through, catching most everyone by surprise. The surfers, almost all of them shortboarders, can't make it over the waves in time, so they jump off their boards and dive deep, still connected to the boards by their surf leashes.

Most California shortboard surf leashes aren't designed for this size surf – as demonstrated by all the shortboards strewn on the rocky beach against the cliff, and all the bobbing heads of surfers as they attempt to work their way back to the shore. Their leashes have snapped under the force of the white water of the breaking waves. Lifeguards are running motorized rescues, using Sea-Doos, as they race around the waves and the white water searching for surfers in need of help.

I'm safe on the pathway high up on the cliff overlooking all of this and I hear a "clunk." I turn to see lying there this dripping wet longboard somebody just plunked nearby on the sidewalk. The board is cracked in the middle and bent like a broken popsicle stick. A guy, in his thirties, still in his black wetsuit, as water drips from it as well as from his hair and nose, sits there sobbing. I understand how he feels. A good longboard can cost over $1000! But he truly looks even more upset than $1000 worth, so I head over to console him.

I offer the standard, unimaginative, "Yuh okay?"

"I was caught inside on an outside set. I dove under and the wave grabbed my board. It wouldn't let go. My leash held. I was dragged under water, must have been a hundred yards, and it wouldn't let go of the board or me! I couldn't get a breath. I thought I was going to drown. It wouldn't let go!"

What do you say to someone in that situation? All I could muster up was, "I'm glad you made it." I let him be.

On that day at Swami's, in those circumstances, even if the lifeguards nearby had spotted the guy face down in the water, there remains the question as to whether he could have been transported to shore and resuscitated in time to save his life.

A longboard with a leash in big waves can really be dangerous. Not only does it do more damage if it hits someone, but it can't pop back through the white water of a forceful wave the way a shortboard can. Also, the longboard leash tends to be thicker and longer and less apt to snap, so it's also more likely to drag the surfer underwater.

What hits me is a "realization", thanks to the event, coincidentally, at Swami's, that surf spot near the Self Realization Center in Encinitas, California. Had one of those outside Hanalei Bay waves caught me, instead of the other way around – had I been stuck in front of a breaking wave or fallen off my board - I might not be writing this account today. Maybe those waves were only half the height of the ones on that special day at Swami's, but this is Hawaii. As I've explained, the waves are different here. The intensity, impact, and raw power of these fast-moving walls of water can't be overstated. I could have easily drowned had my board dragged me underwater in the rolling whitewater.

I'm a lucky guy. I'm lucky because I didn't succeed in paddling into that "Wave of my Dreams" that morning. Had I fallen, or had I not made it over one of those "outsiders," my dream could well have become a nightmare, not only for me...but for everyone in my life.

Some things are just not meant to be.

Thank goodness!

Second Thoughts

※

I was clearly in over my head on that day at Hanalei Bay. In my desire to have a memorable last surf session, waiting for that "One Last Wave," I failed to be certain I was surfing in conditions within my ability range, and that I was surfing for joy, not just for bragging rights to say I went out at Hanalei Bay on a big day.

Sometimes, what we long for, what we think we need, may not be right for us after all. It could be a matter of timing or practicality or judgment. We may yearn for an object like an electric bike or new computer or an expensive dress. Or it may not be a tangible item but instead winning a sports challenge, joining a social group or being with someone you love.

The fact is our needs and our abilities change. It is essential that we keep in touch with the reason for our efforts. We must recognize that in some instances it is better to let go of one objective and move on to another. We shouldn't get so caught up in the pursuit that we lose track of a greater goal...what we truly want or need to accomplish.

Dropping In Deeper

1. What does it mean to "drop in" on a wave?

2. As your mind's eye sees it, sketch what the author sees on the horizon just as he paddles into the lineup or a sight you recall which caused you to become at least a little bit afraid. Be sure to give your drawing a caption.

3. Why doesn't a surfer just ride the wave, especially a large one, straight in towards the beach?

4. Why are the waves in Hawaii so powerful?

5. Since Laird Hamilton is surfing that day, what does that probably mean?

6. Why is the surfer at Swami's crying?

7. What is a deja vu moment, as when Laird Hamilton paddles over to the author for the second time? Maybe you can recall having one. Briefly describe it.

8. The author is very discouraged at the end of this surf day. Should he be? Explain why or why not.

9. Have you ever had a close call? Describe the event and why it happened.

10. Can you think of a "One Last Wave" encounter you have experienced? It does not have to involve surfing, just that kind of situation.

Chapter 19: Longing

– Dealing With Regret & Recognizing Opportunity

"Longing" never seems to jump to the top when you list your emotions or feelings. Happiness or anger or love probably are more likely the ones that come to mind. But longing is very real: you may long to see a special person, miss a particular place, wish for something, or just yearn to be able to relive a consequential moment in time.

Maybe you wish you had shown enough confidence to kiss that girl or realize you could have done more to let your date know you liked him or her. You might have wanted someone you like to have kissed you. Or you might regret that when you were asked to sing, you were too shy. Feelings like these are also longings.

As an unfulfilled desire to go back in time and do something over in a different way, longing often barges into our hearts and minds. It's the feeling of remorse for a misdeed or missed opportunity, of loss that hurts deep inside with every breath when a love affair ends or a loved one, person or pet passes. That sharp jolt of pain throbs with every recollection, a pain like your knees getting slammed together. You feel you'll never again know a time when you can just wake up and smile. But there are ways you can work with longing to keep it from turning into constant regret. You can use it as a tool, instead, to enhance your life.

Pets that were a part of your family for so long are gone. You want them back so badly. The joy, the funny times, and the hassles they created will always remain. The memories linger and this can include, "I wish I had ...taken her to the park more often... put out more toys to make his day fun."

That longing, that wish to have, or have done, even something more in order to feel complete remains, and that's okay. Now, if you get another pet in the future, you'll know how to treat it even better. You've learned that lesson.

The adage, "Time heals all wounds" is true and can help you keep things in perspective. Thankfully, longings and misgivings about past behavior do evolve from being your constant partner to being with you only on occasion. But most times they never fully disappear. It is a Lesson in Life, a difficult one, which remains with you always.

"'Tis better to have loved and lost than never to have loved at all," writes the poet Alfred Lord Tennyson. Indeed, longing can enhance your life by helping you better appreciate present surroundings. You recall what you did have at one time, the good fortune you have known, and how precious each day truly is.

Everyone must endure the experience of loss. It's the price paid for having loved and been loved. Both are part of living. And love will come again. There will be other loves in your life. Guaranteed.

Longing, in less dramatic form, can also occur when you wish you still had that favorite bike or those one-of-a-kind shoes. As you get older you might look back and wish your old hometown could be the way it used to be – less crowded, your best friend still living three houses down the block, that vacant lot you played on with your friends still there…

Longing can also appear in the wish to be forgiven for thoughtless, angry words uttered impulsively. It can be a selfish deed you want to take back or the woeful mistake you would like the chance to make right. You can wish for those things, but you also must accept it can't always be. Sometimes you can go back and apologize to someone, and make things better, but too often, you don't get a "do-over." Did you ever call a friend a bad name, or damage or lose something that belonged to someone else, yet never managed to apologize and rectify things?

Longing can also be for a missed opportunity. You come so close to choosing the better job, a better partner, the right friend, the right thing to say, but you miss the chance and are left with, "I wonder what would have happened if…?" When that guy approached you at school, in front of your friends, and you ignored him because you were a bit embarrassed, you wonder what might have been had you just been friendly to him. That better version of your life remains only in your imagination.

We all have longing in our lives. In school there is no class to help guide you through how to cope with loss and regret even though it's a major part of life. Each person must find his or her way to manage through bad situations and find a new path. In these times, especially, an embarrassing mistake you make can be recorded on someone's phone and put out on social media for all to see. You would give anything to have that erased from everyone's memory - you wish for a miracle.

The following anecdote is just one example of regrets you could someday face as a parent.

Surfing is a devotion, a commitment, and a constant yearning for the high you get when you drop into that overhead, possibly over-your-ability wave and somehow make it! Everyone has some form of the thrill surfers get. It could be skateboarding, cheerleading, or dancing in front of a crowd, horseback riding, acting in a school play, public speaking, etc.

Compare that to being a parent. Parenting is also a devotion and commitment, and, for so many, it also produces those joyful times with your children along with the challenges they present. The difference is that there is an end to the surf session when you paddle back to the beach. There's an end to the school play, the dance number, or the horseback ride. As a parent, there is no paddling back to the beach to end the day. There's no returning to your seat after giving the speech. Parenthood continues with each and every moment.

Now what happens when parenthood competes with surfing or some other passion in your life? The waves are calling, and so is the child! Solution: you take everyone to the beach! This time, that's what I decide to do.

My eight-year-old just-learning-to-surf son sits on his board close to the shore where the little inside whitewater waves roll gently and predictably. I dutifully remain at his side, sitting on my own board, coaching him, pushing him into waves, and sometimes we even catch one together!

PETER MCBRIDE

My wife and our 10-year-old son are on the beach in clear sight, enjoying the day. The warm summer sun shines while the sky remains blue and bright. The rocky shoreline meets the hot sand and it's the perfect picture of summer. Everything is ideal. This is the Life!

Well, almost.

On a good surf day at this beach the waves break further out behind the Rock and are surfable all the way to shore. These are the kinds of waves you put notches on your belt for...the kind a surfer stores away to talk about on another day when the waves are not so great. Not every day is like this.

Today is one of those days, and the surfers are getting long rides. Where my son and I sit, the leftovers of those waves take their last gasp and collapse. There isn't much to them – just a small push of whitewater.

Sometimes, while waiting out by the Rock in the lineup, a wave appears but a surfer passes it up because it doesn't look "makeable" or large enough. Sometimes, after it breaks, the surfer regrets not having taken it because it formed into a much better wave than expected. There's not much of that going on today, though. This is a really good surf day!

Oh geez. My happy kid sits there grinning on his board. I sit there trying not to look at the larger waves farther out by the Rock. It's so tempting to be out there! I'm yearning to be on that wave. I'm longing to have that tale of a wave I can describe on another day when the surf is not so good. But here I am...stuck with my kid.

All I want is just one. Just one wave. I thirst for the thrill of dropping in on that wave, the other surfers' eyes wide-open in awe and jealousy, mixed with a little hope that they might get to see an exciting wipe-out and catch that leftover wave themselves.

I know I can surf these waves today. I grew up surfing here.

My longing turns to lust. Suddenly I'm waving at my wife, pointing to the waves out at the Rock, then pointing at my little son beside me as I hear myself call out, "I'll be right back!"

I know she will keep an eye on him.

Out I paddle, like a fire truck racing to the scene of the blaze. I'm in the lineup behind the Rock now. My wave comes. I paddle into it with all my might.

It's forty-five minutes later and I make it back to where my fledgling surfer son... was. By now he has finished surfing and has joined his brother messing around in the sand. My wife keeps vigil as she sits there beside them. I sheepishly paddle in and resume my role as father. "Hey! What are you guys up to?"

"Hey Dad!" No mention of the surf or my paddling away. It's as if it never happened.

This becomes a part of going to the beach as a family. Routine. It is expected that if it's a good wave day, after a little time spent surfing with my son, I will paddle out to the Rock for my own surf session.

Time goes bye-bye. Many months pass and my little surf partner has moved on and is headed to the baseball diamond or the street to play hockey. In time he's headed to the beach, but now it's with his friends and their families, not with me.

That "routine" with my son, the part where he and I sit surfing together, him depending on me to assist and guide him, will never be again. No longer will he be sitting on his board beside me, near the beach. My other son and my wife will no longer be on the warm sand waiting for me to return from my surf session.

Years and years have come and gone. My son is now in his 30s, and you know what? I can remember that day, and other days quite similar, when I said, "I'll be right back."

It is my personal "Groundhog Day." It keeps replaying over and over in my mind and it never changes.

As I look back upon my behavior, I'm reminded of a YouTube video showing experiments performed on rats. One, presented by Michael Baker, demonstrates how electrodes implanted in the pleasure center of the brain cause a rat to ignore food and water and to instead keep pressing a lever which provides the pleasure sensation. Sometimes those rats keep pushing that lever and ignoring the food and water until they die. They get so consumed by that wonderful feeling that they forget their basic needs and life leaves them.

Am I that rat?

The irony is, I cannot remember even one of those waves for which I left my family in those days. I have no notch on my belt or a surf tale to tell – there is no such memory!

But I know, had I remained there, I would indeed have a father's warm recollections of his son riding white water waves with him or getting pounded and popping up to the surface together! I would have been there to catch a better glimpse of him instead of selfishly riding my own wave, and I would have the rewarding memory of assisting him when he needed my help. These are notch-worthy events!

I long for the chance just to be sitting there once again, by my eight-year-old, helping him and sharing waves with him because he needs me, and I need him. He loves me, and I love him. I so wish to be able to mess around in the sand with my both of my sons and spend quality time with my wife enjoying our beach day together.

It brings to mind Harry Chapin's song, "Cat's in the Cradle" in which he sings about his son asking, "Can you teach me to throw? I said, not today I got a lot to do. He said, that's okay."

Time marches to the rhythm of the future. Thousands of waves have come my way, and I've caught some of them.

Now, however, I realize I let one of the greatest waves of my life -- the opportunity to share in my family's joy -- pass me by without grabbing it.

I will long for that wave forever.

Second Thoughts

※

Think about the opportunities that life presents. Sometimes they're obvious, so easy to see. Sometimes they're subtle and you only recognize them after they have come and gone. Sometimes they're major. Sometimes they're fairly insignificant. No one can master every opportunity that comes their way.

A part of maturing is learning to recognize when opportunities arise, when to act on them and when to just let them pass by. Experience, with the resulting wisdom, helps you learn how to make the best of opportunities and ways of avoiding regret. The longing eases when you find how to make today better through lessons learned from mistakes made in the past.

Dropping In Deeper

1. What does "Time heals all wounds" mean?

2. Is there an incident or relationship you recall that reminds you of a longing of your own? Perhaps it's a time when you left a little brother or sister alone at the grocery store, or something said in anger to a friend. Describe it.

3. Is "longing" the same as "regretting?" Why or why not?

4. You're the older sibling and your little brother or sister tattles on you, leaves messes you have to clean up and hassles you when you are on the phone. Do you think there will ever be a time you will miss this? Why or why not?

5. Sketch a picture of the author and his son sitting in the water with a wave coming as your mind's eye sees it OR a time you did something which you now long to do differently. Write a caption to describe your picture.

6. Could this story go in another direction? Could daughters and sons wish they had made more of an effort to do things with their parents? Give an example.

7. On YouTube listen to the song, "Cat's in the Cradle" by Harry Chapin. What happens in the end?

8. Do you think the author will treat his grandson or granddaughter differently from the way he did his sons? Why and how?

Chapter 20: It's Not Your Fault – *Recognizing And Coping With Alcohol Abuse*

I'm twelve. It's the night following trash pickup in our neighborhood. As part of his service, the gardener put out both of our loaded, dented-up aluminum trashcans yesterday. It's my job to bring in the empty metal cans. Somehow, I have forgotten to do it. They're still sitting by the boulevard at the bottom of our long sloping driveway.

As midnight approaches on this school night, I'm tucked into bed in my upstairs bedroom and well into a second hour of sleep. I have a room all to myself with two twin beds in case a pal sleeps over. It's pretty grand! In the still and darkness, the bedroom door violently bursts open and light from the hallway pours into my startled eyes. The doorknob crunches into the wall, leaving its indentation in the wallpapered lathe and plaster. "You bastard! Bring in those trashcans! Now!"

Welcome to life after 6:00 P.M. at my house. My dad is on the prowl.

Wearing only pajama bottoms, I hustle down the driveway in the darkness, pick up both empty, dented aluminum trashcans by the handles, and struggle back up the driveway with them. I set them down ever so quietly in their place by the backyard gate. I'm rather proud of myself for being so strong - two cans at one time! My dirty bare feet are of no concern. I just want to get back under the covers.

The mood around our house can change drastically. Mom and Dad are typical parents in the daytime hours, making certain we have meals, getting us up for school, and checking if we're doing our homework. Around 5:00 Mom usually manages dinner for my two younger brothers and me; sometimes it's a Swanson TV Dinner, but not usually. She makes a mean spaghetti and meatballs from scratch! But by 6:00 p.m. all of that changes. Mom is upstairs into her vodka, and Dad, arriving home a bit later, goes immediately to the liquor cabinet. Generally, he doesn't prefer beer or wine, though white wine appears sometimes when he eats dinner later. He likes stronger stuff. Unfortunately, alcohol usually puts Dad into a foul mood, and sometimes he goes into a rage.

Here's one example of "the change:" Once, when I'm fourteen, I invite my school buddy, John, to stay over on a weekend night. We've finished a nice dinner that Mom has made and he and I are in the downstairs laundry room getting into our swim trunks so we can dive into the pool. We look forward to swimming in the brightly lit pool water surrounded by darkness. The sight of the backlit shiny bubbles we make when we jump off the diving board at night is pretty spectacular!

As we're still in the midst of changing, Dad comes roaring around the corner into the laundry room, and he's angry! He's upset at me for something, though I'm not certain what it is this time. He raises his hand to strike me, so John and I dodge him and hightail it into the family room and out the back door to the pool. John's only in his underpants. I'm naked. Dad had polio when he was a kid, so he walks with a cane and a brace, but he can still hustle when he's inspired. He chases us by the pool, but we keep clear of him by staying on the opposite side. In frustration and anger, he picks up one of the empty glass milk bottles by the back door and heaves it at me. It just misses and crashes against the chain link fence. After that, John decides not to stay over for that night, or ever again. I can't blame him.

The following morning, I hear Dad coming down the hall. Traditionally on weekday mornings he likes to wake us so we're on time for school. But this is a weekend. Sometimes he climbs into bed with me to talk for a moment. This is one of those times. He tells me how sorry he is for what happened the previous night. Unfortunately, the apology is just for that fleeting moment. The very next night there's apt to be another explosive event. We just never know.

Another time...I have issues. Besides the typical teenage concerns about money for allowance, whether acne is about to attack my face, and hassles with my brothers, I choose to argue with the parents, usually in the evening. One late night Mom is downstairs in the kitchen. She's drunk. She's upset at me for being sassy towards her. I'm unloading on her, complaining about the way things are because of their drinking. I'm standing in front of her, a bit closer than I'd like. We're wedged in between the kitchen sink on one side of the kitchen and the refrigerator on the other. I turn my head for a moment and don't see Mom lean over to reach for her shoe. Suddenly, I'm realizing the piercing pain of her high heel coming down hard on my clavicle, the bone that runs between the shoulder and the neck. It will be several weeks before I feel anywhere close to normal. I have lost the argument.

I know life has been hard on both parents. My little brother was born with physical deformities that not only mess up the looks of his face, but also inhibit his ability to chew food, to hear, and to talk. He's had more surgeries than I can remember, and he must attend a special school for kids with disabilities. This has overwhelmed Mom & Dad. I understand this. But there must be a way we can work things out to make our home life happier. This is my belief.

Undaunted and plain old stubborn, I keep trying to reason with Dad about the drinking and our relationship. I might be fifteen by this time. You see, I really, truly want to have the kind of family I see on TV sitcoms like "The Donna Reed Show" or "Leave It to Beaver." I figure my parents do, too. Maybe we can finally talk it out.

Another night, after Dad has gone through his tirade about the three of us being "spoiled rotten" kids and the yelling and the screaming has subsided, I speak with him calmly just as I'm about to go up the back stairs to bed. I lay out the idea that we must stop this, that we can be a better family, and that we're really good kids, all three of us!

You know what? He agrees! Tears come to his eyes, and he tells me how sorry he is for the way things get at times. He understands what I mean and really wants ours to be a happier family! Progress! He nicknames me "Sunshine" right on the spot. We don't hug at the close because he has a different style. But I do go up to my room with a smile and a real feeling that we've taken a major step in the direction of improving our family life.

The next morning, Dad comes down the hallway for the

customary visit to awaken me. Once again, he climbs into bed with me, though that's not an everyday event. We're talking. I say to him, "That was so great. What you said last night. I think we can..."

Dad looks at me quizzically. "What are you talking about?"

"You know, Dad, at the bottom of the stairs. We were talking and you agreed we could be a happier family...you know?"

"Peter, I don't know what you're saying."

I quickly realize that all of the passionate discussion, the patient reasoning, the love I expressed to my dad that night, and all of those wonderful things Dad said back to me, did not happen for both of us. At that time, I was speaking to a bottle of booze, and that same bottle of booze was speaking to me. Dad is unable to remember anything about our time together.

Please understand, this kind of thing does not occur every night. Oh, the parents are consistent with their drinking, but you just never know when a ruckus will result. It puts a kid on edge, for sure. You just never know what's coming!

I could list many other instances where alcohol abuse interferes with my boyhood. It would not be fun reading. Maybe you can guess why I decide not to even drink wine until I'm twenty-eight; at the insistence of my wife, so I can join her in social drinking. The answer, of course, is that I worry that I might become like my father when he drinks. Fortunately, over time, I discover this doesn't happen. Whew!

I cannot describe the immense weight I feel being a kid and having to manage the abuse in my life that comes from my parents' addiction to alcohol. Their condition becomes more profound from my preteen years all the way until I graduate high school and enter the Navy. I never truly talk to anyone about the matter even though there are two ministers at my church, and I have loads of teachers and counselors at school, as well as friends. The thought of discussing my situation with anyone NEVER EVEN OCCURS TO ME!

My two brothers must cope with all of this, as well. But they're younger and certainly less confrontational than I choose to be. Being the oldest, I forge the way and if nothing else, I make myself the one my parents go after most often when they are drunk. I can see my mom, her face contorted by alcohol and anger, right in front of mine, her spittle sprinkling my eyes, yelling at the top of her lungs, "It's your fault we have problems in this house!" I feel rather like the gang member in "West Side Story" singing to Officer Krupke about all the social issues that turned him into a juvenile delinquent!

But she's not a one trick pony. Other times, in a bit calmer voice, but in the same condition, she spurts out, "Your lips are too big!" Hey! What's a kid supposed to do about his looks? It's not my fault what I look like! Mom doesn't play fair!

It's not all bad, no way! I live in a beautiful house in a wealthy neighborhood, attend a great school with loads of friends, and I'm always able to go on adventures with my buddies. I never go hungry. My parents buy me new clothes periodically. I'm a healthy guy who's active in sports. Fortunately, at age sixteen I have a girlfriend whose mom and dad welcome me into their lives. I feel accepted, loved, and worthy! Her father treats me as he would a son. I'm well off compared to so many others who must deal with an alcoholic parent or guardian and don't have the advantages I know. I believe the person I am to become is the result of the love I feel from my "adopted" parents, as well as my girlfriend. I can't be certain what might have happened to me without them.

But I'm still affected by what goes on at my home after 6:00 P.M. It's fair to say I'm not a "normal" kid, whatever that is. As I said, I have issues, including an extreme lack of self-confidence and the lack of trust that each day will be close to "normal." This affects how I behave, how I respond to people, and the level of maturity I display in my daily behavior.

People choose to drink for many reasons. Some think it makes them more mature and accepted. Others like how they feel when they drink. There's the taste that many find appealing. Drinkers sometimes find it helps them escape from their everyday life for a while. Sometimes drinking changes a person's mood. Others develop an addiction to alcohol and lose control of their drinking, and their lives. For most, drinking can be a pleasant time spent with family and friends, like at dinner or at a bar. It takes on many different roles in our society as people accept alcohol as a part of their lifestyle.

For me, irresponsible drinking leads to many traumatic events in my childhood. And you know what? It's not my fault, but I have a hard time at that age understanding this! It shapes in part the way I develop, some of my attitudes, and what I recall of growing up.

Mine is not a new story. But it's shameful that it is so often repeated generation after generation. It's so hard to break the cycle. But we can minimize the damage of alcohol abuse through education, awareness, and encouraging victims – both the drinkers and their relatives -- to reach out for help and not suffer silently and alone.

Second Thoughts

※

If alcohol abuse or any other type of abuse causes havoc in your life, you do not need to endure the pain alone. Reach out for help. SAMHSA (Substance Abuse and Mental Health Services Administration) has counselors available by phone 24/7 to help. The number is 800 662 HELP (4357), and the website is: https://www.samhsa.gov/find-help/national-helpline.

I just wish I could have known of such a resource back when I felt I had to bear the burden and the pain by myself.

Dropping In Deeper

1. Why does the author's bedroom door suddenly fly open in the middle of the night?

2. What is the meaning of the story's title?

3. Tell about a time you were blamed for something that wasn't your fault.

4. Describe the most frustrating moment the author experiences. What makes it so frustrating?

5. From your mind's eye, sketch the author carrying the two metal trashcans up the driveway in the middle of the night, or the author and his friend as they jump off the diving board into the pool. Include a caption for your drawing.

6. Were the author's parents evil people? Why or why not?

7. What are some of the advantages the author has over many others in his situation?

8. What is SAMHSA?

9. Describe a time you have been startled or frightened. How did

you handle it?

10. Maybe you have faced a time when even though you were underage those around you encouraged you to drink. How did you handle it?

11. What helps the author cope with the treatment he receives from his parents?

Chapter 21: The Best Lesson - *Procrastination & Shades Of Honesty / Favorite Teacher*

They never see it coming. In this ancient rectangle of a classroom nestled above the old indoor swimming pool, the room's bare wooden floors scraped clean of any varnish by the soles of the many souls who have attended class over the decades, seventh graders Tom and Frank slouch in the back corner against the pale faded-blue plaster wall. They sit in their equally old wooden desks with inkwell holes and the carved "hieroglyphics" of past students, who may possibly be grandparents by now. This is an all-boys private school with a history going back to the early 1930s. Tom and Frank are my friends.

In the middle of this room of 20 desks, up against the old slate board, there's a traditional 6" high platform, lifting the teacher's desk and providing him or her a perfect view. The two boys, tucked in just under the classroom flag, heads turned away, leaning towards each other and speaking ever so quietly...are simultaneously thwacked carom-style as a blackboard eraser ricochets off one head and onto the other. Perfection! The flag remains untouched.

A cloud of chalk dust envelops them as their shocked faces turn toward Mr. Best, giving the full attention they have been denying him until now. Satisfied with his ringer of a shot, and without further hesitation, the teacher continues on with the history lecture. Welcome to another day in the life of Mr. Best's fourth period seventh grade History/English class.

Mr. Best is large in girth, rather egg-shaped. But he's no Humpty Dumpty. He can hustle quickly up the stairs every day. Mr. Best is in his late 30s with dark brown hair betrayed by a prematurely balding crown. Sometimes, between lectures about Charles Martel's Battle of Tours in 732 A.D. and vocabulary lessons, we can lure him into talking about his experiences in the Korean War.

We know he knows karate and judo. After he describes using the outward edge of the left hand to strike across the bridge of an enemy's nose, following up with the heel of the right hand thrusting up into the nose, driving splintered bone into the victim's brain...we're certain of his credentials.

Another time, Mr. Best demonstrates a judo move using his thumb and forefinger to squeeze between an opponent's shoulder and neck to induce pain...and surrender. In the future this would become Mr. Spock's "Vulcan nerve pinch" in "Star Trek." Rob, the smallest guy in the class, volunteers himself as a subject; Mr. Best proceeds, continuing to squeeze harder and harder as Rob, aware that the whole class is watching, rebuffs any appeal by the teacher for the "I give" signal. He only offers a half-winced grin. Rob just keeps on taking the pain.

Finally, in an act of wise mercy, Mr. Best relents and gives him an "Atta boy!" nod as he releases his grip. Rob has just moved up one notch on the seventh-grade badass scale.

The whole year we keep asking Mr. Best if he ever killed an enemy soldier. He never answers the question. He only provides a vague, "I just don't know" response. We figure he did.

What he does recall, and requires that we learn as well, is his definition of history. I'm not certain of its origin, but it goes like this: "History is a record of the past which helps us understand the present and prepare for the future." Throughout my life, I'm to think back upon this statement, present it for my own students to learn, and wish that those in charge, our leaders, would use the same words for guidance.

To upset Mr. Best is not the best idea. He's an emotional guy. He turns really red in the face when he's perturbed, as when somebody says something out of turn or makes fun of someone in class. Nobody wants to upset him or, interestingly, disappoint him, either. There is a kind of class camaraderie, a code of honor that we live by in his room. We sport a true respect for the guy, maybe because of the Korean War thing in part, but I think there's something else. As students witnessing his emotions, his sense of humor, and his way of explaining things, we really get the idea he cares about us. That kind of feeling from a teacher doesn't come often enough.

But there is a real problem with Mr. Best. He loves the "Pop Quiz," his unannounced tests.

He also teaches English, with an emphasis on vocabulary. We

get ten new words a week in a workbook, and it seems to us that only a third-year Latin student could decipher the meaning and use of these extraordinary words. Very few of them will I ever come across again in my life! Not only are we to know the spelling and definition and application in sentences, but in a timed quiz we're expected to recognize each word even when the letters are scrambled! This is HARD!

It's Friday. We come in for class with Mr. Best as he waits, seated at his raised desk, for the bell to ring. He stands, points his index finger in the air, smiles and pronounces those two deadly words which always follow the finger: "Pop Quiz!"

We call days like this "Black Friday." For the next fifteen minutes, unprepared as we might be, we madly provide – or make up, definitions and sentences for some of the words. For others, we have to unscramble and then define. It's the usual seventy percent passing requirement. Our hearts pounding, our fingers cramping from squeezing so hard on our Parker T Ball Jotter pens, Mr. Best calls out the dreaded but merciful "TIME!" I have only finished six of them. I manage some wrong answers even in that. I fail. My only solace is that there are a half-dozen others in the class in the same situation.

Assignment: Those who fail must copy ten times, verbatim, the entire definition of any missed words from our Webster's Collegiate Dictionary, including pronunciation guide and parts of speech. I have five to do. Since it's Friday, at least I have the weekend to get the fifty definitions copied, along with the traditional weekend essay due Monday morning. If not completed, the vocabulary assignment doubles. This is, after all, a college preparatory school.

Time passes. It's now 4:30 A.M. Monday morning. My alarm goes off because I have those vocabulary definitions I really should get started on and finish before the school bus arrives at

7:00. Oh, and I have that pesky essay due as well. I can get it done.

Oh bother! And I do mean, "Oh bother!" By 6:00 I'm realizing it takes a lot of time to copy 50 definitions from Webster's. I'm happy to report I did complete that essay, though it's so short one might call it more of a "note to self." I can't get them all done, even with the help of some carbon paper that I desperately and ever so slyly attempt to try out by mixing in carbon copies with my handwritten ones. Mr. Best is going to be so disappointed in me. I'm going to be so disappointed in having 100 definitions to copy!

It's class time later that morning. I haven't been able to eat breakfast. I'm not hungry today. My first three periods have all been spent trying to sneak in a few more written definitions, instead of paying attention. I'm an emotional wreck. It's the combination of flunking the quiz and now letting him down by not completing the weekend assignment.

Mr. Best sits perched at his desk. I trudge over to him, downtrodden like a kid knocking on the neighbor's front door to explain about a broken window, almost working myself into embarrassing tears. But one saving point, one detail that makes it all bearable is, I'm not alone! Steven, the class brain, has failed as well, his first time, and is having his first taste of copying definitions. He hasn't finished, either! We're both in shambles as we approach him, being careful not to step up onto the off-limits sacred territory of the platform.

In this class, everyone carries their books in briefcases. So, from my little briefcase I take out my crumpled mass – or mess-- of papers. Steven does the same thing. We raise our little eyes up to him and I begin to explain, "Mr. Best, about the weekend vocabulary assignment, you see…"

He puts out that large pudgy hand of his, the one we figure has killed enemies using his secret karate moves, and raises it in a traffic cop's "Stop" position. He peers at my little carbon paper-stained fingers as they hold what looks like newspaper trash picked up off the street. I quit speaking in mid-sentence as Mr. Best makes a declaration, a command, I will never forget. He gives me the most important lesson I am to learn in that history class, or that year. It's more important than knowing that Charles Martel stopped the Moors at the Bridge of Tours way back in 732 A.D.!

Heck, it's one of the major Lessons of my Life.

He looks right into my eyes and says the following: "If nobody asks, then don't offer."

"Well Mr. Best, I just wanted you to know that…."

"I said, if nobody asks, DON'T OFFER."

I shut my mouth. I look at Steven. We then look towards our desks. Mr. Best says not another word. We both turn with our bales of trash in our hands, and meekly creep back to our seats.

Mr. Best never does ask for that weekend assignment.

Yes, I flunk another quiz along the way somewhere, but I do pass the class.

And no, I never again wait until Monday morning to begin copying the missed definitions from the Friday pop quiz. Friday evening is as good a time as any to get started!

Second Thoughts

※

There are times in life when saying nothing can be the wiser action to take. Circumstances and the people involved influence the final decision. As to teachers, hopefully we all have a couple of special ones to always remember. Sure, the eccentric and mean ones may come to mind. People are good at remembering bad things. But those inspirational and devoted ones, full of personality, are the ones who deserve our attention. They provide the examples and directions we need to succeed. For the times described here and many other cherished memories, I just wish I had gone back to visit Mr. Best even once and told him what a wonderful influence he has been upon my life, and my career as a teacher.

Dropping In Deeper

1. Why does Mr. Best throw the eraser at Frank and Tom? Do you think this is a good idea? Why or why not?

2. What does the author mean by "the carved hieroglyphics of students?"

3. Describe a time when you waited until the last minute, like the author, to complete something. Were you successful? Did you learn to start projects earlier? What other lessons did you learn?

4. What does Mr. Best mean when he says, "If nobody asks, don't offer"?

5. Why do you suppose Mr. Best never really answers the question about whether he ever killed an enemy soldier?

6. What connection can you find between Mr. Best's backing off from Rob while doing his "Vulcan Nerve Pinch" judo move and letting the author and Steven off the hook when they have not completed their assignment?

7. Is it always a good idea to be completely honest and explain everything? Can you think of a time when it might not be the right thing to do? Explain.

8. What is the saying that Mr. Best teaches his classes? Provide an example based upon events from today, whether from your own experience or headline news, where you can apply this saying.

9. Have you ever known a teacher you respect the way the author and the class respect Mr. Best? If so, what makes that teacher so special?

10. Sketch the class with Mr. Best at his desk, as your mind's eye sees it OR the Tom and Frank event with the erasers. Describe your picture with a caption.

Chapter 22: Heavy-Duty - *Feeling Lost, Alone, Hopeless / Happy Ending*

I'm sorry. I must apologize for the hard realities that we, your parents and caregivers, have left at your feet…realities you have to deal with on a daily basis. I imagine many of you must feel overwhelmed right now – lost and unsure of what direction to take and wondering what will be tomorrow. You might feel like what's happening in the World today grabs at you, tosses you about, and won't let you go, like the worst wipeout of your life while surfing. To live in today's World has become a heavy-duty experience.

The problems I know as a teenager and young adult in the 1960s and 1970s cannot compare to the challenges you face presently. But I do have one unique concern that you don't have to manage: the military draft. Learn a Life Lesson from this heavy-duty story:

Half-way through my 17th year, I graduate high school and that fall I follow the crowd into college – junior college for me. I may know how to study, but I don't want to. I'm content surfing, working a part-time job at a gas station, and spending quality time with my high-school girlfriend who's soon to become my fiancée.

When a guy turns 18, he MUST check in with the Selective Service (the draft board) a federal government agency that registers and takes young men to serve in the military for two years. During the time of my eighteenth birthday, if you maintain passing grades in college, you receive a 2-S deferment from the draft, meaning Uncle Sam will wait until you finish college and THEN take you away to the Vietnam "Conflict" – an undeclared war we're fighting in some faraway place for reasons we don't understand.

A year later, my grades reflect my unwillingness to study while I focus on surfing. I can't explain why I choose to be so lazy and make myself a target for the draft. I understand that I'll have to leave school, my girl, AND SURFING, but I just don't give a damn. I'm crazy but it's just the way things are. There is no doubt Uncle Sam will be calling upon me very soon.

I discover that instead I can enlist in the Navy for a six-year reserve program which requires I go to monthly meetings and bootcamp the first year, active military duty for two years, and then attend meetings and two-week summer drills the following three years. Oh, and if there's some national "emergency", since I'm a reservist, I could get called back to duty. However, it's the Navy reserves, so I figure I'm safe from crawling and fighting in the jungles of Vietnam. The six-year commitment sounds like a better deal to me. I sign up and on September 17, 1968, at age 19, I go active duty.

Now we move ahead to the spring of 1970. At 21 I find myself onboard a ship in the middle of Vietnam's Gulf of Tonkin. I'm on water, not "in country", so at least that part of my strategy has worked. There are 650 other guys with me onboard, yet I feel alone and lost. It's all because of "Mail Call."

When you join the military, whether kicking or screaming because you've been drafted, or you have enlisted, Uncle Sam owns you and every day of your life. These days he usually sends you overseas to Asia to join in the fracas in Vietnam. You cannot head back home. You have no passport, little money and, if you were to somehow jump ship, the authorities would track you down in short time – in Asia, unless you're of Asian descent, you stand out. It's a trap and you can't escape until Uncle Sam decides it's your time to head home.

I know guys who have had their enlistment extended, against their will, because there was a shortage of personnel with their specific skill ("rate"). It's just the way it is. My specific skill is surfing...combined with maybe a little guitar and singing. I figure that isn't a "rate" the military would want to keep around any longer than necessary – I want to be as valueless to the U.S. Navy as possible. "This is a good strategy!" I tell myself.

It's April of 1970 and the upcoming mid-September end to my two years of active duty approaches so slowly. The Vietnam War pounds away just a few miles across the water. I'm onboard a fast combat supply ship, the U.S.S. Sacramento (AOE-1).

As we churn through the waters in the Gulf of Tonkin, an aircraft carrier, 3-½ football fields long (a bit longer than the

USS Sacramento), and a destroyer, much shorter, pull along each side of my ship. We sail in parallel lines as cargo cables and oil hoses connect the two ships to ours while helicopters hoist and transfer pallets of ammunition, oil, explosives, food, and supplies from the USS Sacramento to the others.

As I watch this amazing feat, I am reminded of a time a group of us were on the freeway in two cars with boards stacked on top, headed back from the beach. While cruising down the highway at 70 mph, the cars maneuvered in close to one another so we could toss one guy's forgotten disposable camera through the window of the other car. We didn't want to have to bother to stop to make the exchange. It worked! But our one-time successful venture can't compare with what these Navy ships do each day.

Later, two more ships may come alongside to repeat the process. This will happen numerous times over the next several weeks until the USS Sacramento's supplies are depleted. Then we return to Subic Bay in the Philippines for a few days to stock up, only to shortly return to our place "on-line" back in the Gulf of Tonkin.

I wish to break away for a moment to explain something – why I find myself not in a totally reasonable, positive state of mind. I'm thinking rather erratically during my time on the USS Sacramento. The term, "irony" applies here.

One form of irony occurs when the truth, what develops in the end, contradicts the expected outcome. For example, the "unsinkable" Titanic ends up hitting an iceberg and going down to the ocean bottom on its very first voyage! That's ironic. I wish to share an example of irony here from my time in the Navy. It will help you better understand how upset, frustrated, and lost I'm feeling, and why I behave as I do, especially toward the end of my enlistment.

A year prior to my present situation onboard the USS Sacramento, I have been assigned to Midway Island Naval Base, located in the middle of the Pacific Ocean. It's a small island (actually two atolls). I could walk around the main island, Sand Island, in a couple of hours. Because Midway is so far west and close to the International Date Line, we're the last place on Earth to celebrate New Year's Eve or the Easter sunrise service.

After finishing my assigned job in the communications center, and on weekends, I often work for extra pay as a lifeguard on the shoreline of the Officers' Beach. Families gather there to play in the sun and swim in the aqua-blue waveless water (a barrier reef blocks waves from crashing on the shore.) From my 6' high tower I can see Navy ships on the horizon, headed west to Vietnam. I am thinking, "Those poor guys. Here I sit, basking in the sun on a tropical island with women and children all around. I'm watching these ships head to war. I'm so glad I'm not in their shoes." Life is good on Midway.

Less than a year later I happen to walk back to the fantail (rear) of the USS Sacramento to which I've been assigned. We're on course in the mid-Pacific, headed to Vietnam. I look out and what do I see? I see Midway Island just a few miles distant, beckoning to me to return – with all the memories of gooney birds, A7 jets, and the communications center – oh, and that beach where I was once the lifeguard. There's probably a lifeguard on that beach right now looking out and seeing my ship journeying west – to Vietnam. I bet I can imagine what that lifeguard is thinking. What an ironic situation I find myself in! I'm not happy about it.

The most essential item for the servicemen, mail from back home, gets transferred from our ship to the one alongside during underway replenishment. It hangs from the cables connecting our ships in dirty gray U.S. Post Office sacks. The pulley system guides those bags across the blue, 85-degree water to anxious hands onboard the receiving ship.

I've seen that cable carrying a mail sack droop down to the frothing water of the gulf as we rise and drop over large ocean swells. Over the din of whirling helicopter blades, conveyor motors, forklifts, and ocean swells pounding against the sides of the ships, I have heard the anguished screams of carrier crewmembers as they witness the carnage, the destruction of their beloved mail.

Unlike today with email communication abilities, "snail mail" in the 1960s is the lifeline of every soldier, sailor, and aircrew member. The letters and care packages tether military personnel to the love and promise of home and family, no matter what chaos the military throws at us. Whether I'm assigned to mid-Pacific Navy base Midway Island, or a year later onboard the Vietnam-bound Sacramento, when "Mail Call!" sounds over the base or ship's speakers, hope and childlike glee rise like cream to the surface of my mood. I live for Mail Call. We all do.

My fiancée writes at least a couple of times a week. Her letters, sometimes enclosing the pink lipstick imprint of her lips so sweetly placed just below her perfumed, "With all my love, Jane," often arrive in clumps of mail written five or more weeks apart - along with a stack of the hometown newspaper I subscribe to but rarely read. I quickly learn I am never to receive even one issue of my Playboy magazine subscription. Someone else in the military snags it first.

Looking forward to Mail Call can be like waiting for the next good-sized swell to hit my home break. My anticipation erupts into sheer joy when that swell arrives and I can get to the beach to snag a few great waves. Mail Call, just like the next big swell, is not consistent or predictable – at best it's eventual. Both help me keep myself whole and give me a purpose for carrying on to the next day when there just might be another letter from her, or, if I were home, another day of fine waves.

We go on-line in the Gulf of Tonkin for several weeks, replenishing the carriers and destroyers assigned there. As a member of the deck crew, I work in my blue oil-stained dungaree uniform, helping connect oil hose lines to be hoisted over to each ship that comes alongside. Our ship eventually returns to the Philippines for several days to stock up with fuel and supplies and then does the turn-around back to the Gulf.

To break up the monotony, we do make brief R&R (rest and recuperation) jaunts to Yokosuka, Japan and Hong Kong, China during our "Westpac 1970" tour of duty. Almost everyone makes it back to the ship safely after going on liberty in Olongapo (Subic Bay) or one of the other ports o'call. Sometimes things happen. You never know.

Lately I've noticed the letters from my girl, the ones she's been writing for the last year and a half, are arriving less frequently – and don't say much. Her mom's letters, which come occasionally, are now more apt to be the ones handed to me at Mail Call. Something's wrong… When we come into port at Subic Bay, I spend my entire paycheck making an overseas phone call to Jane. "Are you okay?" I ask. "How are you?"

"I don't know," she mumbles, not saying much, but I can hear her sobbing.

"What's wrong?"

"I don't know," she manages again.

"I'm returning as soon as I can!" I reassure her. We will repeat this performance, and I will spend my whole paycheck in this fashion, numerous times over the next couple of months.

During my entire time in the Navy, I've resisted spending much money so I can save for our wedding day and beyond. When we're in port and go on liberty, while my buddies party, I'm the guy who stays sober and helps his mates return to the ship. While my deck buddies' names appear on the Report to Sickbay List – requiring they check with the corpsman to be sure they've recovered from whatever they came down with after going ashore - I'm the guy who never messes around and whose name never appears on that list. I have a fiancée back home!

The Navy allows up to three months "Early Out" for personnel accepted into college, and since my enlistment ends September 17th of this year, it's perfect timing! Indeed, as Jane's letters arrive less and less often, I'm filling out an application for Santa Monica City College summer school. My true purpose, of course, is to return home to Jane as soon as possible and save our engagement.

But I'll tell you, I'm ready to study now. I've made A's on a number of college correspondence courses while in the Navy. I'm inspired by the guys onboard who I NEVER want to resemble in any way – the ones with the coffee cups hanging from their belt as they belch at me their next command. I figure a college education will protect from that.

My acceptance letter arrives. The Early Out requires approval from the commanding officer. I put in my request with a copy of the acceptance letter, but I hear nothing back. I'm told, "The request must have gotten lost." I put in another request, hear nothing again and, after one more attempt and a few weeks more of waiting, finally receive the word: "Request Denied."

My crew chief pulls me aside. "Pete, the executive officer handles crew matters, and he doesn't believe in Early Outs for education."

Yikes!

Jane's parents have always treated me as their son. We're quite close. Her mom writes that Jane's dad has contacted our senator in Washington about the matter. I must compose an explanatory letter to the senator, and he will investigate. This is great!

I send the letter to Jane's dad who forwards it, with one of his own, to Senator Murphy. After no word over the next couple of weeks, I decide I'll speak to the captain myself! I request a Captain's Mast to do so. In this situation the crew member stands before the captain and/or the executive officer while either answering to punitive charges made against that crew member or speaking about a personal matter of importance. At this "hearing" I ask, "Why has my request to attend college been denied? The Navy says I may end my enlistment early if I've been accepted, and I have been!"

The captain replies, "Seaman, we see you've written to Senator Murphy. You have quite a way with words. We can use you in the writing of the ship's cruise book (yearbook). You'll be transferred to work under the chaplain. You will write for the cruise book, help organize the crew's library, and assist with Sunday services."

There goes my "strategy" for being as valueless to the U.S. Navy as possible. That's it. No Early Out. I'm no longer a member of the deck crew. My workstation and battle station during general quarters now is the library. Get this: even during GQ drills (the signal for the crew to prepare for imminent danger), as the battle guns fire away shaking the entire ship, my duty, my military responsibility in time of possible attack, is to run around the library making certain books don't fall off the bookshelves!

A few weeks later I receive a letter signed by the senator detailing what I already know, and informing me, "…because you are assisting with the cruise book, library, and religious services, you are deemed essential to the crew's morale. Therefore, I can do nothing to further assist you. Thank you for your service to our country as a member of the U.S. Navy."

Oh God. Please help me. Yes, I can describe how I feel right now. It's like standing in shallow water off the ocean shoreline and having a huge wave build up in front of me and break, pounding me to the bottom and continuing to mash me down with a constant current of water. It smothers me, much like a 300-pound wrestler sitting on my back as I lie face-down in the sand, never letting up. I can't catch my breath. I can't say, "I give." I'm dying. This is how it feels right now. Do you ever feel this way? I KNOW I must get back to my girl. But I've done everything I can think of to make that happen and I've failed. I'm in a prison as she fades away from my life…I don't know what to do! I'm losing everything. I'm so lost. Everything is out of control.

The calendar crawls to June. This is when I should be home attending college and hanging with my fiancée. Instead, I'm in the Gulf of Tonkin tending to a library which few crew members even use. Worse than that, Jane has completely quit writing. My only letters at Mail Call now are an occasional one from her mom telling me nothing, and some occasionally from my little brother or my best friend. As far as I'm concerned, Mail Call is my personal ghost town. There's really nothing to look forward to when the mail announcement sounds – except a pile of weeks-old newspapers.

I struggle. I'm a zombie. I've lost spirit and all hope. I'm depressed, though I don't understand the term. I do my jobs like a robot. Imagine me as a small metal ball bouncing all over in a pinball machine, flippers knocking me against bumpers and propelling me as I crash into everything on the pinball board. All I want to do is go straight down the hole into the belly of the machine and lie quietly. But that can't be. Whoever's playing knows the game well. I'm caught in this never-ending cycle and I want out! God, please help me. I want out!

It feels like my worst-ever wipeout surfing as white water thrashes me about, throwing me to the bottom, my worthless arms flailing against the smothering foam and grinding force of the relentless wave. It won't let me go. I must get to the surface somehow!

There's no one I can find to talk to about my ordeal. The chaplain is a cold-soul of a man in his 40's putting in his time until he gets shore duty to be with his family. He doesn't need me to help with religious services because he already has a younger assistant (who could give lessons on how to be unfriendly). I do little more than tidy up the library. I'm basically a hot turd dropped in the chaplain's lap that he must deal with however he can.

The lieutenant in charge of the cruise book has me write some descriptive paragraphs about the different departments onboard. I research the departments and finish that task in a week. There's no real reason I can't attend college summer classes...except for the "Stop Sign" put up by the ship's executive officer.

The guys I know onboard from my time on deck crew get their excitement talking about our next stopover in port, getting drunk, and meeting women. That's not what I want to talk about right now. I begin to ponder maybe just letting go...maybe I run and dive off the bow of the ship while we're cruising in the gulf – if I don't drown immediately or get churned up by the ship's propellers, the sea snakes will finish me off.

It's so hard. There are other guys I know receiving "Dear John" letters from girlfriends breaking up with them long-distance, and they work out a way to handle it. Time heals all wounds. They're clear on where they stand and what the situation demands of them.

But to be uncertain…to hold the hope that maybe I'm misunderstanding things, maybe there's a good reason for the letters stopping; has she really left me for someone else and that's the way it is? Oh man! I'm so miserable! I'm so confused! I spend my free time, which is most of the day, studying a college correspondence course or learning new songs on my guitar. I'm alone most of the time. It's almost like solitary confinement in a 15' by 30' cell – but it's a library. I write lost-love poems and put them to music – this is my salvation. I grew up Episcopalian, but I just don't see God answering my prayers right now.

While I'm feeling so sorry for myself, there's no denying how fortunate I am compared to the guys our efforts support – who are based "in country" in Vietnam. They're just trying to survive another day in the jungle without getting killed or maimed, awaiting the time when the powers that be release them to return home. Many of them have had their love letters stop, just like mine.

But it's all relative. Back to surfing: When you surf, you usually sit for a while, waiting in fairly calm waters for the next set of waves to arrive. If it's a day of big surf and you spot that first huge wave on the horizon, the adrenaline flows and your heart pounds like crazy as you paddle towards it. But if it's a "tiny" surf day, the waves being only 1 to 2 feet and only arriving every 15 minutes or so, you know what? As you sit in that calm water and peer out to see a 2-foot wave finally approaching, the adrenaline can flow just like on a big day, and your heart pounds like crazy as you fiercely paddle for it! It's nuts. It's exciting! It's addictive.

I think anyone who fishes can relate to this – the adrenaline rush of catching a marlin while deep-sea fishing can be the same as the feeling during a slow day of lake fishing and pulling in a fair-size trout. Someone in sales knows the thrill of "landing" a big account compared to garnering a small piece of business after a long dry spell. It can be the same thrilling feeling in all these circumstances. It's all relative.

The amount of misery the guys stationed on land must endure – if they're able to survive the war conditions surrounding them – will change their personality, their outlook, and their attitude towards life forever. It's like surfing a day of giant waves and barely surviving a traumatic wipeout. It can change a person.

What I'm going through, though paltry in comparison to the circumstances surrounding a guy "in country", still changes me. My situation onboard is heaven compared to their hell. But the intensity of my loss and feeling abandoned as my love letters fade away, devastates me just the same. This is my present state of mind. I'm unable to step back and take a wider view of the predicament and compare it to that of others. I don't appreciate the many ways I have been so lucky.

Mid-June comes around and I get some form of the flu. It's severe enough that my lungs crackle when I breathe; I have a fever. In sickbay we only have corpsmen onboard. Doctors are only available on the aircraft carriers.

I report to sickbay late one morning and the corpsman deems me ill enough to qualify for transport to the USS America to see a doctor. That's the aircraft carrier we are replenishing at that time. He fills out a form and I report to the deck to be transferred over. They load me into a cage attached to one of the over-water cables and off I go, just like those bags of mail!

I make it to the carrier, just like the mail usually does. It occurs to me as I land on the terra firma of the other ship that perhaps I should have informed the chaplain. But in my present state of mind, being the pinball that I am, the surfer hopelessly enmeshed in a wave which won't let go, depressed but not even realizing it, I give it a little wince and figure that the form they filled out will cross his desk or they will contact him – after all, they sent me. Besides, I'll certainly be back before too long. He probably thinks I'm still in the library. No big deal.

Life on the America is amazing! As I head down to sickbay, I stop to peer out at a jet launching from the flight deck. It's right out of the movies! I'm enjoying this illness I have! Sickbay has a long line of fellow sailors waiting to be seen. I start to wonder how much longer the two ships will remain alongside one another. Normally, the entire process of replenishment takes several hours – usually the full morning or the full afternoon. But I'm not too worried. "Something will work out," I say to myself.

It's at least an hour until I see the doctor. Then I proceed with a sputum sample and examination; he gives me an antibiotic, and...all done! Up I scamper to the deck to be reloaded into the cage. Whoa! There's no ship alongside! The USS Sacramento has departed...without me! What to do?

I wander around for a while, watch jets take off and land, and just sort of explore the ship. I'm really in no hurry to remind anyone I'm onboard. It's so much fun!And I've had no fun for so long. There are thousands of men on the USS America, most of them dressed in their blue denim work jeans and shirts like mine, so I blend right in. It's wonderful! I find the crew's mess and enjoy a meal and then, as night falls, decide I should let someone know I have been left behind. It's not my fault the line was so long at sickbay. I don't know who to tell, so I return to sickbay to check in with them. Here I am, that pinball bouncing all over the board, that helpless, hopeless surfer, but I'm having a good time! It brings me joy.

Nobody says much to me. "Report to berthing quarters and they'll give you a bunk." But first I can't resist heading up to take in night-time flight operations – what a show! Eventually I make it back down and a guy assigns me a bunk. It's nice... except for the shipboard sounds above of jets launching with the help of the steam-driven cable system.

The next morning, after a pleasant breakfast, a petty officer approaches and tells me, "You'll have to wait until we're alongside the Sacramento again – day after tomorrow. In the meantime, you have free time. Just keep out of the way."

Super! This is such as great time! I'm feeling better and everything is an adventure! I spend those two days just taking in the sights – day and night launches and landings, a wheel coming off one jet as it takes a hard hit on the flight deck... a burial at sea for someone who has died onboard. The USS America is a small city with 5000 inhabitants and things happen. It has its own zip code! I get to observe life there as a visitor. I don't waste much time sleeping. It's a fantastic distraction from my "normal" life onboard the USS Sacramento and the torment I feel.

As they say, "All good things must come to an end." We pull alongside the USS Sacramento right on schedule two days later and shortly I'm bobbing up and down in the transport cage, heading back to "terra bummer." Little do I realize just what a "bummer" it's going to be! How was I to know the chaplain

DID miss me later that afternoon and did NOT get the form explaining that I was sent to the doctors onboard the USS America? He initiated a ship-wide search for me and the captain presumed me to be LOST AT SEA! The chaplain personally went through trials of his own spirit and faith attempting to figure out how this could have happened to the seaman for whom he was responsible.

Well, I DO find all of this out when the normally mild-mannered chaplain explodes while I sit before him in front of his desk. It's probably fortunate for me the desk is between us! He goes on quite a tirade, ending with, "I'll probably write a book about this someday." With that, he concludes saying, "Seaman McBride, you're no longer assigned to the library. Report immediately to the crew's mess."

It's all gone...library duty and GQ station, working on the cruise book, and assisting with Sunday services. My status as "essential to the crew's morale" takes an astonishing turn. I'm now, "essential to the crew's meals." Up to now I have been fortunate, and rather proud that during my entire time in the service I've never had KP duty (kitchen police). You know, it's that "lowest man on the totem pole" job of peeling potatoes and swabbing the mess hall deck and washing dishes – usually assigned to brand-new recruits for their first two or three months onboard. Well, that's now my job...for my last three months...when I should be in college and back with my girl!

Shortly I'm promoted to working in the chiefs' mess, a smaller eating area exclusively for chief petty officers. It's considered an honor to work there with fewer crew members to feed and a compact space to keep clean. If a person handles things right, the workday is shorter than it would be in the crew's mess. I learn these guys are really picky about their food, and I'm responsible for cooking their morning eggs and toast EXACTLY the way they want them. If it's "sunny-side-up," that egg had better look like the sun. I work at this for a couple of weeks and get pretty good at keeping the chiefs happy...most of the time.

I dedicate myself to this task and I'm proud for what I'm managing to do here! But things change one morning when one chief orders two eggs "sunny-side-up."

"Ah, that's my specialty!" I think to myself. I serve them to him and they're both perfect – like sunshine. When I go to retrieve his plate, he has mangled one egg, half the yolk smeared all over the plate with shreds of his buttered-to-perfection toast, and he has put out his cigarette right in the middle of the bright-orange yolk of the uneaten one. I'm not discouraged. I'm disgusted!

I request a transfer back to the crew's mess. It means later work hours, more tasks, and a larger deck to swab...but I won't have to take a personal interest in how food is prepared or eaten. That is a relief!

Late at night, just after closing down the mess hall, a few of the older crew members routinely gather at one of the crew's mess tables to drink the last of the coffee from one of the giant urns. I notice when they put their cup under the spout and pull the handle, the stuff oozes out, looking more like Hershey's chocolate syrup.

One evening I can't resist asking one of these crusty guys, you know, tattoos on both arms and a cigarette clenched between his orange teeth, but quite friendly, "Why do you guys wait so late to have coffee?"

"Ah, 'cause it tastes best right at this time of day," he replies. This all becomes a nightly ritual. I keep that one urn turned on just for these guys. You can tell they appreciate it. I'm pleased about that. They eventually struggle up and straggle away. It's now my job to wipe down the table, take care of their dirty cups, and clean out the giant coffee urn. As I proceed, as I scoop out the last of the liquid and sludge at the bottom of the urn, I can't help but notice, every night, the three or four boiled cockroaches floating around in the blackness.

"Mmmmmm." But I never tell the guys...it would ruin it for them.

The letters from my girl, my fiancée, never arrive again. I accept my fate. Survival means living on the hope that somehow things will work out once Uncle Sam releases me on September 17th. I remain faithful to her and the dream.

Okay, I do somehow meet a Chinese girl in Hong Kong when we make a port o'call there that August. I'm so lonely, and she's cute and speaks English with a British accent. I take her to dinner... yup, Chinese food. It's remarkable that after dinner, close to midnight, the streets are jammed with people as if it's noon! They tend to walk with their hands clasped behind their backs. It may be so they don't knock against someone else's hands because with so many people about, they must pass by one another quite closely.

I walk her to her front door, say a gentlemanly, "Goodnight!" without kissing her (I don't have the nerve), turn and attempt my gallant and memorable (right out of the movies) exit... as I fade into the crowd along the sidewalk. Unfortunately, as she is watching (no doubt, I imagine, with a tear in her eye), I immediately step off the sidewalk to give way to the oncoming pedestrians – and squish my left shoe into some dog poop. A refined shake of that shoe, a practiced scraping of the sole against the edge of the curb, and I'm on my way back to the USS Sacramento!

Because of the bombs and nuclear armaments we carry onboard, our ship must moor a mile outside of Hong Kong Harbor. The small ferry requires over twenty minutes to take us from the dock to the ship. As we get underway early the next morning, I stand in the fantail area watching the city fade from view. Suddenly, I feel that urge to dive off the ship – not so much, this time, to let go of my life, but to swim back to her, my dinner date in Hong Kong. I know I'm in love... When you're this lonely, and away from home for so long, it's so easy to think you've found someone.

September 17th arrives, and as it happens, things do work out! Two weeks before that day, the Navy releases me from the USS Sacramento and flies me back to Long Beach, California. I go through the process of being honorably discharged.

Upon my return, I contact Jane and discover she has a new boyfriend who works in her office. He's older and knows how to wine and dine her, impressing her in a way I never could manage at 19, nor yet at 21. Things take time. But I do get my engagement ring back. They eventually marry. We all move on.

I take the opportunity to ask her, in person, "Why didn't you just write me a Dear John letter so I could know what was going on?"

"Well (she starts that sobbing, again) ...I thought you might do... something desperate." She believes that if I had known I had lost her, I might have done the unthinkable.

Yup! She's right! I might have...after getting over the initial shock, like so many other guys I know onboard had to do, and accepting the reality of how things stood, I might have spent my paychecks on something other than overseas phone calls! I might have partied more in the bars in Subic Bay...in Yokosuka...or with the girl I took to dinner in Hong Kong. Who knows? I might have joined my buddies onto the "Report to Sickbay List "- the one that comes out just before we pull into port!

I'll never know. But I do know, if only there had been someone I could have talked to about things while I was onboard ship, I could have appreciated how fortunate I really was - much sooner than I eventually did.

Second Thoughts

※

On November 22, 1963, in the middle of his physiology lecture, my high school teacher, Mr. Holtfrerich, is called to the door and quietly given a message. He returns to his desk and solemnly announces, "I've been informed that President Kennedy has been shot." Shortly after that announcement we are released for lunch where we learn our very popular and charismatic president is dead. Everyone wanders about in a daze.

Our World turns upside down that day. It never returns to normal, especially since within five years, Dr. Martin Luther King and presidential candidate, Robert F. Kennedy, brother to President Kennedy, will both also be assassinated. These events, along with the draft in support of the war in Vietnam, hang over our heads every day. They become a part of our everyday thinking and routine.

In that state of mind, I find myself lost and unaware when I go over to the USS America. I am that pinball, bouncing around on a gameboard of depression, the surfer lost in a wave that won't let go. Maybe you feel that way right now. This can happen at any age, but it's especially common in the late teens and early twenties.

If you were in my situation, you might find some of the activities I choose, the guitar, the poetry, the college courses, workable. Or you might find other activities to help you survive. Reading, joining others for card games, taking pictures, sketching, and studying a foreign language come to mind.

Writing about how we feel and what gives us hope might help. Religious guidance is another resource. We must do something.

Most importantly, reach out for help. Talk to someone. Don't keep your worries and frustrations deep inside you – share them with someone who cares. These days SAMHSA (Substance Abuse and Mental Health Services Administration) has counselors who can guide you to someone who can help, and they are available by phone 24/7.

The number is: 800 622 HELP (4537), and the website is: https://www.samhsa.gov/find-help/national-helpline

I wish I had known way back then if there was someone, some organization, available to help me.

Dropping In Deeper

1. What is one "heavy-duty" concern of the author and those of his generation? What makes it such a problem?

2. At the time of the story, why is Mail Call so important to those serving in the military, especially overseas?

3. When the author states, "Mail Call is not consistent or predictable – at best it's eventual," what does he mean?

4. Name something in your life that might have similar importance to that of Mail Call in military life. What makes it so significant for you?

5. As your mind's eye sees it, sketch the mail bag traversing along the connecting cables from one ship to another or the author in the ship's library during GQ or the author as he leaves the girl in Hong Kong. Stick figures are fine. Be sure to include a caption which explains your drawing.

6. What was not available to help the author through his difficult time that young people going through an emotional crisis can access today? How do you use it?

7. It was irresponsible and stupid for the author to not tell the chaplain that he was going over to the USS America. Why didn't he tell him?

8. Have you ever known the terrible feeling of something

missing from your life as when the letters for the author stop coming? You don't have to say what it was. What way did you find to cope with it?

9. Would you have told the crew about the roaches? Why or why not?

10. What is your opinion? Is it worse for the letters from someone you love to just stop with no explanation or to just receive a "Dear John" letter – telling you the love affair is over? Why?

11. What do you suppose you would you do if you know a close friend suffers from a broken heart – an ended romance? There is no one answer to this question because circumstances and personalities can be so different.

12. Name one lesson you take away from this story.

ACKNOWLEDGEMENT

Thanks, CAROLYN GROGAN, for reviewing my first drafts and providing guidance and encouragement in the writing of this book. AMY HARNED, I appreciate you patiently reading through and locating the typos and "misplaced modifiers." JAYNE WALLACE, you combine editing prowess with that attitude of yours full of cheer and reassurance. GAIL MARCHI, your candid observations about chapters of the book helped me turn the corners and find the straightaway. JENNY KELLERHALS, you showed me the way to organize and prepare the text for distribution and find the ways to reach those who would benefit from this book. STACIE HUNT, you inspire my every day and accept my very early morning "productive time" as part of our wonderful relationship.

Again, thanks to all of you, and those who inspired me through our relationships and experiences as we "dropped into" and shared some of the Waves of Life together.

Photo Credits

Chapter 1: Sheila in Red - *photographer unknown*

Chapter 2: Avalon Monster - *Peter McBride*

Chapter 3: Smokey - *Robin Davis (used with permission)*

Chapter 4: They're Out to Get Me - *Rich Ruiz (used with permission)*

Chapter 5: Bridging the Gap - *Photo Courtesy of Total Escape* http://www.totalescape.com/outside/campsites/kings-river-camping/

Chapter 6: Bodies Surfing - *Peter McBride*

Chapter 7: The Incredible Shrinking Boy - *Steve Deppler (used with permission)*

Chapter 8: George - *Peter McBride*

Chapter 9: Frenemies Forever - *Paula Bickford (used with permission)*

Chapter 10: Sidehill Badger - *photographer unknown*

Chapter 11: Submarines, The Silent Service Days - *photographer unknown*

Chapter 12: County Line - *Peter McBride*

Chapter 13: Crossing a Stream - *photographer unknown*

Chapter 14: Social Experiment - *photographer unknown*

Chapter 15: Luck Wears a Veil - *Paul Bickford (used with permission)*

Chapter 16: Billy Bully - *Paula Bickford (used with permission)*

Chapter 17: The Gift - *Paula Bickford (used with permission)*

Chapter 18: Close Call - *John Culver (used with permission)*

Chapter 19: Longing - *Mindy Hartshorn (used with permission)*

Chapter 20: It's Not Your Fault - *Rich Ruiz (used with permission)*

Chapter 21: The Best Lesson - *Jill Wilcox (used with permission)*

Chapter 22: Heavy-Duty - *Photo Courtesy of The Washington Post*

Author's Page: *Ryan McBride (used with permission)*

ABOUT THE AUTHOR

Peter Mc Bride

Eldest of three boys whose father was an orthopedic surgeon, the author lived in a secluded wooded area of Georgia through age 5. It was a time of segregated schools that he did not understand and close calls with snakes that he did. A move to the Philadelphia suburbs came next with its, "Hey yo!" culture, insulting one another by using hand gestures while making bullying a sport. He did not participate. But those first-snow mornings were unforgettable and the three-story brick school buildings were magnificent places of learning.

At age 9 the family moved to Los Angeles where he attended a college preparatory school for boys until ninth grade and then a public high school. He made life-long friends at both. Football and swim teams, along with surfing, were his passions. Two years in the Navy followed, and then several years as a traveling program director for Los Angeles Schools. Along the way the author earned both his Bachelor of Arts and Master of

Arts degrees as well as two teaching credentials, was honored as "Student of the Year" at California State Los Angeles, and taught at numerous schools, public and private, elementary, and secondary. He was also a traveling educational speaker for University of Phoenix.

He married, has two grown sons, and is now a grandfather. Presently he works with his wife in their media production company and does voiceovers. Through Arts for Learning in San Diego, he has enjoyed presenting stories and songs to children in schools and libraries. Though retired from teaching, with guitar in hand, he finds substitute teaching a few times a month rewarding, especially when a student asks, "Will you be here tomorrow?"

The author has two sayings which he considers precious and have guided him throughout his career and life: "It's for the kids," and from the Disney movie, Dear to My Heart, "It's what you do with what you got." Though "got" is, admittedly, a vague, non-descriptive verb, he hopes what you "got" from reading this book makes a positive difference in your life and in those around you!